PRACTICAL RISK MANAGEMENT

by

J. E. BANNISTER

and

P. A. BAWCUTT

LONDON
WITHERBY & CO. LTD.
5, Plantain Place, Crosby Row,
London SE1 1YN

Published 1981

1st Edition

Reprinted 1982

©

J. E. BANNISTER
and
P. A. BAWCUTT

1981

ISBN 0 900886 22 6

PRACTICAL
RISK MANAGEMENT

FOREWORD

Risk is an ingredient of all human life. How best to live with it is a problem for every individual and indeed every enterprise. Only in the past twenty years has it come to be recognised that the management of risk, which everyone practises to a greater or lesser degree, can be put on a systematic basis so that possible losses from the occurrence of untoward events can be minimised or provided for in optimal fashion. Hence the term 'risk management' which has been a subject of the curriculum at City University Business School since 1972.

Early teaching was of necessity based on American texts. There were no others available. Now Jim Bannister and Paul Bawcutt have spared time from their busy lives as practitioners to provide us with a book that synthesises theory with practice so that it will be of value not only to students but even more to businessmen and their advisers who need to put theory to effective use in their affairs. Their current account of risk management is no mere academic exercise. Every page bears the mark of having been written from a wealth of experience. As examples one need only mention, first, the approach to loss prevention and, second, the problems inherent in the formation and operation of captive insurance companies.

A refreshing feature of their book is that they do not claim to know all the answers. They invite criticisms and suggestions. The subject is a developing one. But in the present state of the art there are no surer guides to the practitioner or the student than Bannister and Bawcutt. Read their work, practise what they preach, and you will be well on the way to minimising the cost of risk for your enterprise.

Hugh Cockerell

City University Business School
Gresham College
Basinghall Street
London EC2V 5AH.

PREFACE

Risk management has sometimes been described with a degree of accuracy as "applied common sense". So why should we treat it as a separate subject?

The timing is not accidental. Throughout the last hundred or more years commerce and industry have become more detailed, many businesses have grown to enormous size, and jobs have become more specialised. It has been a time of great technical achievement but not without cost.

The occasional major disaster in the air, at sea or on land, the growth of crime, including both violent and white collar crime, and the problems of avoiding political and social disruption nationally and at the level of the individual enterprise, illustrate the problems.

Risk management has evolved as a series of techniques borrowed from other disciplines for handling the increasing uncertainties of commercial, industrial and even political life today. It has been applied to reduce substantially the cost of on-going regular loss and as a consequence often to reduce the cost of insurance. More important, it plays a growing role in reducing the possibility of disaster whether from sudden physical loss or from other types of threat.

There has been an attempt to present risk management as a new discipline, which is a mistake. It works best when added to the other tasks of the line manager by focussing on recognising future uncertainty, thinking through its possible manifestation and effects and devising plans to reduce its impact on the individual or organisation. It must include assessing the range of possible financial variation and making sure that provision has been made to handle this fluctuation in financial performance by insurance and other means as appropriate.

Risk management can be sophisticated and complicated but the starting point should always be a simple assessment of the problem and possible solutions. Over-complexity can make the problem worse—it can increase the threats to success. Often it is necessary to work in considerable technical detail but only when the broad situation is clearly understood and overall objectives defined.

In writing this book we have therefore been concerned both to present a broad philosophical and conceptual approach and to demonstrate its practical application. It reflects very much our own experience in working with

vi

clients in many industries in many countries on practical risk problems and developing solutions in joint work with them.

Many friends throughout the world have helped to shape both thinking and content. We are grateful for large numbers of talks, sometimes looking at risk management in a broad context, but often tackling a specific problem. These discussions have helped us to build a framework which has been used in the risk management courses presented in many countries.

It has been most encouraging to see how widely risk management is considered as a complete or partial answer to managing future uncertainty. We both have an insurance background. This should logically lead to a focus on the assessment and management of risk both technically and financially. Regrettably there is still inadequate attention to risk evaluation and control in the insurance world.

This book uses an approach that is often insurance related. Talks with scientists, engineers, psychologists, sociologists, economists and others have both contributed to a broader understanding of risk and shown that risk management is not and cannot be the sole property of insurance companies, insurance brokers and insurance buyers.

Risk management is still evolving quite rapidly. The bulk of the material in this book was written in 1977-1978. It has been updated as far as we are able in terms of fact, but should be regarded as a provisional textbook of risk management. We expect risk management to change.

The checklists in the appendices were originally prepared by Hugh Spencer and we are very grateful to him.

Finally, we must thank all who have helped us—colleagues, clients, professional contacts and acquaintances. We would welcome comments.

Jim Bannister

Paul Bawcutt

Risk Research Group Limited, Bridge House, 181 Queen Victoria Street, London EC4V 4DD

CONTENTS

APPENDICES

CHARTS AND DIAGRAMS

Chapter I

Risk Management

1.1 What is Risk Management?

"It is a world of change in which we live, and a world of uncertainty. We live only by knowing something about the future; while the problems of life, or of conduct at least, arise from the fact that we know so little. This is as true of business as of the other spheres of activity. The essence of the situation is action according to opinion, of greater or lesser foundation and value, neither entire ignorance nor complete and perfect information, but partial knowledge".*

That quotation from one of the classical economic textbooks of over 50 years ago, shows the ubiquity of risk. It is everywhere and in every activity. We can comprehend it to some extent but if we were able to comprehend it completely, it would not exist. For without uncertainty, there can be no risk. Equally, without uncertainty, ours would be, as Professor Knight points out several times in his book, a boring and indeed a completely unliveable existence.

Risk has been part of man's whole history on this planet. For our Stone Age predecessors, risk could be seen in terms of wild animals, failure of food supply, lack of food for other reasons, loss of dwellings through catastrophe, or attack by other men and groups of men. Those hazards are still with us today, although in different form. In Stone Age times there was a great deal of uncertainty in man's existence, but most of the uncertainty was in timing. Man was aware of the possibility of each of the major hazards but he did not know when and where they could strike.

---

* "Risk, Uncertainty and Profit", Frank H. Knight, Boston, Mass. Houghton Mufflin Co., 1921.

Subsequent history shows a greater and greater impact by man on the risk characteristics of his own environment. Meteorological and other environmental change unrelated to man's activity has been of relatively little importance. Most of the changes in risk and uncertainty have been due to man's impact on his environment and his fellow men.

The very dispersal of Stone Age man, his relative independence of other men and a relative abundance of natural resources in relation to his needs meant that the management of risk was very much a personal affair. To the extent that it required co-operation with other men at all, this was on an entirely local basis.

The development of society and economic systems since prehistoric times has been paralleled by a growth in man's dependence upon systems. Our dependence is still increasing at a faster and faster rate. We depend on highly complex and highly vulnerable systems for all of the necessities of life except air. This exception is a somewhat negative one as, even in this case, we are dependent on man's activities not polluting the air we breathe beyond acceptable limits.

Looked at in terms of the necessities of life, such as heat, light and shelter, we are dependent on other men and on systems for providing them, which are vulnerable to instant disruption, whether from strike or property damage. In the industrialised countries, there is hardly a single individual who could feed himself unaided. Today he is dependent upon lines of production and distribution.

It is against this background of systems vulnerability that the need for organised risk management has become self-evident. Despite the knowledge explosion, most risk management is not planned but reflects a response to events after they have happened. Large-scale catastrophes tend to overwhelm our capacity for realistic response. The only answer is in better planning and preparation to manage risk.

From a wider point of view, a new and more far-reaching reaction to systems vulnerability is the beginning of a tendency away from size for its own sake. It is now increasingly recognised that economy of scale produces much greater exposure to risk.

The dangers of faster and faster change have been discussed in a best seller by Alvin Toffler.

"Eons ago the shrinking seas cast millions of unwilling aquatic creatures on to the newly created beaches. Deprived of their familiar environment, they died, gasping and clawing for each additional instant of eternity. Only a fortunate few, better suited to amphibian existence, survived the shock of change . . . To assert that man must adapt seems superfluous. He has already shown himself to be among the most adaptable of lifeforms. He has survived equatorial summers and Antarctic winters. He has survived Dachau and Vorkuta. He has walked the lunar surface. Such accomplishments give rise to the glib notion that his adaptive capabilities are infinite. Yet nothing could be further from the truth.

For despite all his heroism and stamina, man remains a biological organism, a bio-system and all such systems operate within inexorable limits.

Temperature, pressure, caloric intake, oxygen and carbon dioxide levels, all set absolute boundaries beyond which man, as presently constituted, cannot venture. As when we hurl a man into outer space, we surround him with an exquisitely designed micro-environment that contains all these factors within liveable limits . . .

. . . There are discoverable limits to the amount of change that the human organism can absorb, and that by accelerating change without first determining these limits we may submit masses of men to demands they simply cannot tolerate. We run the high risk of throwing them into that peculiar state that I have called future shock. We may define future shock as the distress, both physical and psychological, that arises from an overload of the human organism's physical adaptive systems and is decision-making processes. Put more simply, future shock is the human response to over-stimulation."*

The inclusion of that quotation is intended to illustrate that the management of risk is the universal problem, a problem for each and every one of us in his day-by-day life at work and play. The study of risk and the management of future uncertainty is therefore one of the most important topics for each of us.

This book is not concerned with the wider aspects of management of risk, although they are mentioned in order to put the subject in proper perspective. Essentially, in this book, we are concerned about techniques for managing risk in business.

Until recently, there has been a dichotomy in the treatment of risk in business. The handling of what has been

---

* *Future Shock: Alvin Toffler, New York, Random House, 1970.*

called "commercial risk" has been kept quite separate from the handling of what is called "insurable risk".

In one of the most widely quoted textbooks on risk management the scope of risk management is defined as follows:

"Businessmen face two kinds of risk: dynamic and static. Dynamic risks, often called speculative risks, arise from unexpected changes in the economic productivity of a given capital investment.

They arise from market, management, and political sources and are ambivalent in nature: they can result in profit as well as loss. Static risks, often called pure risks, arise independently of the movements in the economy. They arise from loss of, or damage to physical assets, loss of possession of assets by fraud or criminal violence, loss of ownership by adverse judgments at law, loss of income resulting from damage to property of others, and loss of net income owing to the death or disability of key employees. Static risks, unlike dynamic risks, can lead to losses only. Profits are not a result of assuming a static risk.

Static risks are more subject to scientific control than are dynamic risks. The growth and development of the economy, however, depend on the existence of an adequate number of investors willing and able to assume dynamic risks. With dynamic risks, individuals might suffer a loss from a situation that results in a gain to society.

Some risks are worth taking; others are not. The difference lies in the size of potential losses, in the excess of gains over losses, and in the favourableness of the odds. Beyond this, it is a matter of knowing what the real potentials are and of being properly prepared for all of them."*

However, only a handful of pages in that particular book examine commercial risk as distinct from insurable risk. The authors state in their preface that the term "risk management" has not been in use long enough to have an established definition. They compared men in top management positions who dealt with risks every day in their efforts to create profits for stockholders and who looked upon the whole of corporate management as risk management, with others who took a narrow view of risk management and used the term to define the activities of the corporate insurance buyer. Mehr and Hedges settled for taking a position that risk management, as a managerial

---

* *"Risk Management in the Business Enterprise"*, Robert I. Mehr & Bob A. Hedges, Homewood, Illinois, Irwin. 1963.

function, was something more than corporate insurance management and something less than all management. They defined risk management as "the management of those risks for which the organisation, principles and techniques appropriate to insurance management are useful".

Sixteen years later that definition looks unreasonably narrow. Despite the efforts of many insurance specialists to contain the subject of risk management to the insurable risk area, to the average businessman such a separation is impractical. The narrow view which has prevailed for a very long time of insurance as a separate discipline, as a subject only for the specialist and as far too complicated for the ordinary businessman to understand, is being rejected categorically.

Insurance expenditures are too big to be delegated to a relatively junior executive. The risks to which the corporate enterprise is subject are seen more and more by businessmen as an intricate whole. For some of them, insurance is available, and for some of those risks for which insurance is available, it is an appropriate technique for the large or medium-sized business.

A great deal of the impetus for this comprehensive view of risk is coming from younger financial directors, particularly those who have undergone lengthy training at business schools. Financial directors of this kind analyse all expenditure in terms of resources committed against return. It is a short step from such a cash flow analysis to the concept of "trade-off".

Trade-off is a difficult concept for an insurance man to understand, and some other businessmen have difficulty in comprehending it theoretically, but each of us is involved in trade-off decisions of one type or another day by day. By "trade-off" we mean the commitment of resources now, against the expectation of future higher returns. For a commercial risk situation, trade-off means usually capital investment now, against the expectation of a potentially high return in the medium to long term. For insurable risks, trade-off means the payment of a premium now, against the expectation that if a defined loss is suffered, financial recompense will be forthcoming from the insurer. In the insurable risk situation, we use trade-off as a means of reducing financial uncertainty. The promise of the insurer to pay gives us reassurance and enables us to deal with a situation of financial uncertainty.

In a commercial risk situation, we accept uncertainty in the expectation of reward. We assume that we have the capability to manage the risk implicit in that future uncertainty better than our competitors, so as to derive from the future situation a higher return.

Having looked, albeit very briefly, at the general topic of risk and insurance, we ought to try and define risk. The biggest problem we face is that the word "risk" has been used in many different ways. A number of mathematicians, statisticians and economists talk about risk as covering a wide spectrum between certainty on the one hand and certainty on the other. Uncertainty in these circumstances has often been defined as complete ignorance. Frank Knight defined uncertainty as existing when there is more than one possible outcome to a particular course of action, the form of each possible outcome is known, but the chance or probability of getting any one particular outcome is not known. He went on to say that if the probability of actually obtaining certain outcomes was known, then the situation would be one of risk, not uncertainty. Most economic textbooks deal with risk in this connection in terms of illustrations with the throwing of dice.

This presents the student with a dilemma. The essential work on analysing the probabilities of throwing a dice was in fact carried through by Galileo Galilei some 350 years ago. His analysis is used largely unchanged in many works covering statistical probability.

Unfortunately, when one reviews the work of economists and others, there is a gap between the essentially theoretical view of probability, risk and uncertainty and the real world. If one accepts the differentiation mentioned earlier between risk and uncertainty, the only situation that would qualify for being described as a "risk" would be that of dice throwing and similar games of chance. Any attempt to relate dice throwing to activities with more human variability would seem to be doomed to failure.

Therefore we would argue, in conflict with a number of eminent economists, that risk is in fact uncertainty, or more correctly uncertainty about the possible variability in result (due to uncertainty). Some of this uncertainty has always been present as in the illustration, earlier in this chapter, of Stone Age man, but a great deal of our present uncertainty is the direct and indirect result of man's activities in all its complexity. We would therefore suggest as a definition of risk the following:

"Potential variability in the future outcome (of a stated situation) due to uncertainty."

The definition, sounds too much like jargon but it does contain the essential elements and brings risk a little nearer to the ground. First of all it talks about variability in outcome; secondly, it talks about the need to relate any examination to a specific situation so as to examine how that situation will change; and thirdly, it gathers together all the factors that will change under the general heading of uncertainty.

To resolve uncertainty completely is neither possible nor desirable but to understand the situation in which such uncertainty is a factor is possible, at least in broad terms, and such understanding brings with it first of all the capability to survive in both physical and economic terms and secondly the possibility of physical and economic advance.

We should move on from a consideration of risk to the aims and objectives of risk management. Peter Drucker has commented on commercial risk as follows:

"To try to eliminate risk in business enterprise is futile. Risk is inherent to the commitment of present resources to future expectation. Indeed, economic progress is defined as the ability to take a risk. The attempt to eliminate risks, even the attempt to minimise them, can only make them irrational and unbearable. It can only result in that greatest risk of all: rigidity."*

That comment may be a little frightening to the would be risk manager but Drucker goes on to say:

"The main goal of a management science must be to enable business to take the right risks. Indeed, it must be to enable business to take greater risks—by providing knowledge and understanding of alternative risks and alternative expectations, by identifying the resources and efforts needed to achieve desired results—by mobilising energies for contribution; and by measuring results against expectations, thereby providing means for early correction of wrong or inadequate decisions."

That comment is a good summary of the concept of commercial risk management.

---

* Peter F. Drucker, "Management Tasks, Responsibilities and Practice" London, Heineman, 1973.

It is necessary to use a somewhat wider approach for a comprehensive system of risk management, embracing commercial and insurable risks, and a definition we might use is:

"Risk management may be defined as the identification, measurement and **economic** control of risks that threaten the assets and earnings of a business or other enterprise."

The word "economic" is emphasised to put a limit to risk management activity which otherwise could be unending. One prominent insurance broker has described risk management, with some justification, as positively the longest piece of string he had ever seen. The point he was trying to make is that there seemed to be no end to it. Such unending risk management would be totally unacceptable to business management and the community at large. By using the word "economic" we can limit our activities to those that pay for themselves in terms of ensuring that the real saving from the risk management activity is greater than the losses avoided. To avoid any confusion, we are not talking about potential losses avoided, but actual losses avoided. This means that we can measure the effectiveness of our risk management by a reduction in the cost of losses. Where losses are frequent, it will be possible to measure and indicate an improvement resulting from conscious risk management activity. Where we are protecting an enterprise against a catastrophic failure, it will not be possible to evaluate risk management on the basis of a reduction in cost of loss. In most cases the catastrophe will not occur anyway. We are forced in such a situation to rely on more subjective judgment of the utility to an individual or an individual board of directors of a reduction in the expected probability of catastrophic loss.

One other distinction needs to be made in relation to the definition. As stated, it does not include the possibility of applying risk management to non-profit making activities. We can deal with this eventuality by altering our definition to read as follows:

"Risk management for non-profit making bodies may be defined as the identification, measurement and economic control of threats to the continued provision of essential services and supplies."

1.	PHYSICAL LOSS OR DAMAGE TO PROPERTY—Injury/Death	
2.	LIABILITY—Suits from customers/ employees/public	Potentially at least partially manageable (and insurable)
3.	BUSINESS INTERRUPTION—Loss of earnings from physical or other loss	
4.	MANAGEMENT—e.g. Poor planning control, staff selection etc	Directly controllable by management
5.	WASTAGE—e.g. Poor packaging stock control, deterioration, corrosion etc.	
6.	TECHNOLOGICAL—e.g. Change reducing demand or profit, failure of new technology	Not directly controllable by management
7.	SOCIAL—e.g. Change in habit less product demand, more vandalism	
8.	POLITICAL—e.g. Government, legislation, pressure groups especially inflation, foreign exchange risk	May have positive or negative effect
9.	PHYSICAL ENVIRONMENT—e.g. Climate, depletion of resources	Manageable to greater or less extent

CHART 1. A CLASSIFICATION OF RISKS

1.2 Types of Risk

Chart 1 gives a somewhat arbitrary classification of risks. It is not intended to be all-embracing and there is scope for many different views in the make up of such a table.

The first risk listed is that of **physical loss or damage to property** and **injury or death of people.** Many of the obvious areas of insurable property risks are covered by this category. It would include fire, lightning, explosion, flood, windstorm, and impact damage to fixed or moveable property. The loss or damage to property may be accidental or deliberate. Under deliberate loss we would certainly include arson and fraud, but in fact, we are considering any type of loss of assets by partial or full loss.

The second category is also easily recognisable as an insurable risk—the risk of **liability** resulting from suits from customers or employees or the general public, who feel that they have suffered loss or injury as a result of an individual's or a company's activities. Apart from awards against the individual or company, such a heading can include the necessary legal cost of defending such actions or answering complaints from customers and others who feel they have been wronged.

Business interruption, or as it is more usually called in this country, consequential loss, means any loss of, or shortfall in earnings resulting in physical interruption of production. We should note that we are not concerned only with physical interruption within the premises of a particular company, but we must also concern ourselves with interruption at a customer's or supplier's premises, if it is sufficiently important to affect our earnings. As far as customers are concerned, not every interruption or misfortune to the customer is necessarily a misfortune for us; his loss may mean an additional order for equipment or machinery or stock. If, however, we are manufacturing or handling an initial or intermediate product which our customer's factory then subjects to further processing, the loss of this factory by fire may mean that he is unable to accept the expected volume of our product and we will suffer a diminution in earnings.

These first three categories cover broadly the range of risk for which insurance offers financial protection. In general terms, individuals or companies can protect themselves to a large extent against this type of risk. By ensuring that we do not bring together sources of ignition and goods that will easily burn, we can reduce the possibility of fire hazard. Similarly, by making sure our electrical systems are in good order, we can further reduce the risk of fire. We may choose to supplement our precautions by having available fire extinguishing apparatus, either manual, in the shape of portable extinguishers and hoses, or automatic, in the shape of sprinkler and drenching systems. Our propensity to property loss may also be reduced by the training and motivation of the workforce. This training can include instructions on taking care of property, fire fighting and recognition and handling of hazards.

However, all of our precautions may be thwarted by a determined arsonist or by a combination of the circumstances leading to a loss. We should not give up, however, because one can be aware of the possibility of arson and the techniques available to the arsonist. By strengthening our protection, we may make it difficult for him to enter and difficult to gain access to vulnerable plant and machinery.

Similarly, by taking care in the manufacture of our product, its labelling and instructions for use, by training distributors and salesmen to carry that care through into the sale of the product and by monitoring the performance of the product when used by customers, we may be able to reduce the incidence of liability suits. It may still be impossible to prevent them occurring and there is room for loss control in the shape of speedy recognition of customer complaints, with the object of turning an aggrieved customer into a happy customer so that not only do we reduce the possibility of a legal claim, but we turn the customer's original complaint to marketing advantage, as he recognises our concern for his problem.

The third area is also open to loss control initiative. By analysing the dependency of important sectors of our earnings on critical items of plant or machinery inside and outside our works, we can take measures to reduce the dependency. Contingency planning can give the capability to recover more quickly from a potential disaster.

In each of these three areas, our biggest problem is to recognise and anticipate the threat or combination of threats that may cause us injury or damage. To the extent that we can successfully identify the threat, it may well be possible to manage it. In the chart, we have described these three categories of risk as partially insurable. At first glance, it may be felt that such risks are completely insurable but examination of the small print in most insurance policies will reveal that exclusions of one form or another limit the cover, so that many may not be fully financially protected against the impact of such risks.

Moving down the table, we come to two categories of risk that are directly controllable by management, namely **errors** of **management** and **wastage.** We have selected, as illustrations of management risk, the results of poor planning, poor control and poor staff selection, each of which may cause a variation in our expected result. In considering the impact of quality of management on risk, we are not concerned only with negative events. The full range of possibilities is from superb, above-average management to very poor, inadequate management. When considering planning mistakes, the impact of those mistakes may come quickly and be relatively small, or it may be delayed and be catastrophic. Lack of adequate control in a management risk may mean that many other risks are run unwittingly and in an uncontrolled fashion. Poor staff selection can also result in many different kinds of loss. It will be recognised that this particular category, like every other category, can have an impact on other types of risk, so that together they produce a situation and the loss that would not have happened on its own without both being present. For example, poor staff selection may result in a disgruntled employee who is more likely to burn down the premises or permit the premises to be burnt down.

Wastage is not always thought of as a risk but it will be seen that wastage does result in both small and large-scale uncertainty. Small-scale uncertainty, can be the results of poor control manifesting itself in deterioration of product, corrosion of vital machinery or pipework, loss of stock through inadequate stock control or inadequate or inappropriate packaging, and may lead to damage to the product or an item of equipment destined for a factory.

In these two areas, we thus have the small regular type of loss which may become an accepted part of the industrial scene and the irregular and rarer situation where the lack of effective control results in a more serious loss. (Corrosion in pipework will ultimately lead to physical loss of the pipe but if this is carrying a dangerous liquid or gas, the effect of the corrosion loss will be multiplied many hundreds or thousands of times).

These two areas of management and wastage are particularly appropriate for risk management treatment because they are directly controllable. In many companies, they are also significant sources of loss and often the loss from these causes is many times the rate of the loss from what are considered insurable events.

The last four categories in Table 1 relate primarily to events outside the company, although the company can to some extent take advantage of the opportunities those changes offer and minimise the disadvantages implicit in them.

Technological change illustrates the contradictory positive and negative aspects of risk. The growth of a new technology, such as the introduction of digital display watches, may produce an outstanding new commercial opportunity for the company that has the right resources and capability but can be a significant threat to an older industry, in this case the mechanical watch industry. When dealing with this type of risk, one is making a judgment, first on the physical aspects, and second, and much more important, on the reaction of sectors of the population to those events. It is also necessary for the company to be able to assess its own capability accurately. It may be felt that there is a vital need to develop and introduce a new technology but if the risks in that decision are not properly evaluated, the misjudgment may cause the company disaster.

A good example of this type of risk has been the crisis in the aircraft industry resulting from new engines. The development of the Rolls Royce RB-211 engine at one point outran the financial resources of Rolls Royce who had need of government aid, not only to continue the RB-211 project, but to stay in business at all. If Rolls Royce had failed; the future of the Lockheed Aircraft Company would also have been in doubt, as its then new aircraft, the Tri-Star, was dependent on the RB-211. New problems may be expected when new technology is introduced and if the time-scale is misjudged, the delay of months or even years may bring bankruptcy to the company or even the industry concerned. It should be noted that we are talking about two kinds of impact from technological change. First, the impact on existing business through reduced demand following the successful introduction of a new technology by a competitor and second, the risk implicit in placing great reliance on new technology and then being unable to produce the required goods or market in time.

Social change is a major factor in risk. Throughout history, social change has always been with us but, equally, it has occurred at a relatively slow and therefore more easily manageable rate. In the last 30 years, the impact of television and other means of instant knowledge has led to faster rates of change, not only of fashion and other cycles being faster, but also changes that might well have been thought unthinkable a few years earlier. Among the changes that are particularly relevant to risk today are an increasing alienation from work, less concern for private property, more reliance on government and the creation of sudden demand for new or existing products. It is questionable whether the electronic calculator has made or lost more fortunes. At present, we can see examples of both in companies that have judged or misjudged the demand and the production potential. The world-wide use of jeans has affected substantially the demand for other clothing whilst making fortunes for manufacturers of denim cloth.

Social change, manifesting itself in urban decay and the growth in violence and vandalism has resulted in increases in property loss, caused partly by the direct results of violence and vandalism, partly by lack of attention resulting from changed social views, and partly as a result of police preoccupation with other more serious crimes.

Companies and individuals are highly vulnerable to **political risk** or changes in legislation or attitude resulting from the action of governments or other political bodies. Some of these changes are very direct. An example is inflation resulting from inadequacies of government and the resulting foreign exchange risk, as markets endeavour to readjust to differential values and more important, to estimates of different future relative values.

Apart from the impact of inflation and foreign exchange risk, political effects are manifold. In most countries, the volume of legislation is increasing year by year, imposing greater cost on business in conforming with the legislation and resulting in restraints on previous freedom to operate commercially. The uncertainties in relation to future government action pose a major threat to most businesses. During the past few years political risk management has developed as a technique both for understanding these changes and for beginning to cope with them.

Although the impact of **environmental risk** is not new, it is potentially far more dangerous today as a result of the changes man has made to the surface of the earth. Storm, flood, ice, snow, together with earthquakes, volcanoes and tidal waves, have been present throughout man's history on the planet and for long before. When populations are scattered and man's investment in buildings and equipment are small and fragmentary, the impact of natural disasters is relatively limited. The grouping of populations into cities and the steady increase in both complexity and dependence on systems, have meant that the modern world is much more vulnerable to environmental impact than during man's earlier history. Total reliance on electrical and other large-scale systems can lead to death and privation from cold, hunger and disease in time of emergency if adequate contingency plans have not been developed. In surveying our somewhat arbitrary classification of risks or threats under the nine headings in Chart 1, one should bear in mind the important inter-relationships between each type of risk. They are not isolated, separate threats, capable of being dealt with one by one. As well as analysing the threats individually, we need to take into account their inter-reaction and make plans to deal with the failure of systems.

A hypothetical example may illustrate this interdependence. Imagine an explosion at a chemical works producing a chemical that is dangerous to human and animal life. First of all, there is a substantial property loss; second, there is an interruption of production and third, there is the possibility of liability suits. However, the impact of this particular threat does not end there. Dissatisfaction amongst customers and the public at large may lead to legal and political demands for changes in the company, even to a boycott of the company's products, and may even require the prohibition of the use of that particular technology. This increasing systems vulnerability underlines the need for creative risk management, not to eliminate risk, but to make possible the controlling of its negative effects and taking of opportunities related to its positive effects.

This classification also shows the distinction between what have been loosely described in this chapter as commercial and insurable risks. Items 4-9 in Chart 1 are clearly in the commercial risk area, whilst items 1-3 are in the insurable risk area. We have seen that there is at least theoretically a relationship between the size of uncertainty and the potential profit from successfully "managing" risk.

In commercial risk management our aim must therefore be to take the right risk, which is the risk where our skill and resources produce the best profit potential. This may arise because of our knowledge, because of our equipment, because of our reputation, because of our staff, but in every event, it will be individual to us. It will be a special combination of skill and resources that enable us to take this opportunity successfully. It will be appreciated that the translation of that opportunity into profit depends, first on the recognition by others of our capability and second on our ability to produce the desired result.

The best profit potential will also vary according to our personality, either individual or collective. Some individuals and some companies are happiest when taking risks; they actively seek opportunities to use their skill in taking and managing risks. Others, of more cautious frame of mind, pursue a different target, that of minimising risks and of seeking to avoid any peril or danger. It is probably inevitable that the risk seekers have the possibility of greater rewards, but also a greater possible variation in the future outcome of their ventures. Those seeking a less risky activity will spend more money avoiding risk, will be less competitive in seeking areas to take risks, and will, in general, enjoy a lower return than their risk-taking competitors. Again, theoretically, we can compare the small safe return with the large unsafe return. In making such a comparison we are looking forward into the uncertain future. When we look backward at the results of such activity, we may find that the picture has been reversed. The apparently small safe return has produced a larger profit than the large unsafe return. In a particular case it is not too clear whether the failure results from our incompetence or from luck. As Frank Knight put it:

"There is in the exercise of the best judgment and highest capacity an inevitable margin of error. A successful outcome in any particular place cannot be attributed entirely to judgment and capacity, even taken together. The best men would fail in a certain proportion of cases and the worst perhaps succeed in a certain proportion." *

In trying to establish the nature and character of commercial risk we must inevitably start with some simple basic assumptions. All business and commercial activity involves the sale of goods or services. When we decide individually or collectively to enter into this activity our selection of the type of business, its location, the method of manufacture, distribution and selling, the price and payment method, all involve risk. We can, to some extent, perceive and understand this risk from our present knowledge and similar businesses. However, we can be threatened (or more positively, gain opportunities) from future changes in our environment. Most of those changes are proceeding without any impact from our activity but each of our actions does have an impact large or small on our environment. In trying to analyse future uncertainty, we are examining a near-infinite number of actions and reactions taking place between an almost infinite number of people and things.

Our **selection of the type of business** we engage in reflects our risk personality. It may be a stable and apparently reliable business with a comfortable and unexciting future

---

* Frank H. Knight, op. cit.

ahead of it. It may be a business with tremendous potential but still relatively new and untested. It will therefore have the potential of tremendous reward or large-scale failure. The type of business we enter will involve us in greater or lesser capital resources. Here we are concerned, not only with the size of financial resources but the time-span of return. There is a very great difference between a very large expenditure with a very fast return and a similar large expenditure with a very slow return even if the present cash value of both streams of earnings is similar. The advantage of the fast return is that our uncertainty tends to decrease as we reduce the time-span of our activity. We can talk with greater confidence of what will happen in a few months' time than of what will happen in a few years' or a few decades' time. Some business decisions are instant; others require a commitment now in expectation of a return in 10, 15 or 20 years time, as with a new major power station or similar utility.

Location is a major factor in commercial risk. We may choose to serve a relatively narrow market near to us; indeed, we may have no option if our product is a bulky cheap one. Or we may choose to serve distant and wide-spread markets. We may enter an area where the characteristics of the product and its consumption mean that we can have a virtual monopoly over a small geographical zone, or we may be joining with many others competitors in serving the same area. We may be protected from competition by distance, or exposed to it because the transport costs of the product are insignificant.

In determining the **method of manufacture,** we are of course equally varying our exposure to risk. Mass production means the commitment of large resources to manufacture before sale, on the assumption that buyers will be available at the right time, in the right quantity and the right price. In making to order we may eliminate the risk of having unwanted products, but at the expense of losing many sales because the customer is not prepared to wait. We have a similar choice in distribution. We may choose to sell direct with all the additional work and complexity it gives for the possibility of a higher margin and greater control of how our product reaches its customer. If we feel that our particular risk skills are in the production area and not in the marketing area, we may prefer to leave all the selling and distribution to a specialist wholesaler or distributor, in which case a critical system dependency for us will be the relationship with that wholesaler or distributor particularly if there is no alternative.

Our **pricing decisions** also involve considerable estimation of risk. There is usually a relationship between price and volume and the character of that relationship will depend to a large extent on the competitive position in our market. This may result in a relatively narrow envelope of sales volume and price at which we can make profit or give us the opportunity of selecting from a large range of price-volume trade-off decisions.

In deciding the **method of payment,** we equally face risk decisions. Pre-payment reduces a great deal of the financial risk, although we may be subjected to subsequent unrecoverable increased cost of production. Once we give credit, we automatically expand the risk of our business and the credit may be controlled or uncontrolled.

In some businesses, the answer is a form of delegated credit where an external body provides credit for one's customers. Although this removes some of our risk in that we are not then having to find the cash to finance the purchases in order that our customers can make them, it introduces a new dependency because the sudden withdrawal of credit or the inefficiency of the credit supplier, or a change in style of the credit supplier, may suddenly and unexpectedly threaten our business.

As we have seen earlier, every business decision involves this element of trade-off, an expenditure now against an expectation of future profit or an expenditure now to avoid future larger possible loss. Each of our trade-off decisions reflects our view of future uncertainty (what we think will happen) and our risk philosophy, (whether we are comfortable taking risks or avoiding them).

Every product and service sold or bought includes two major utility elements, the reduction of risk and the provision of the service. The proportion of each utility element in the price varies according to the activity concerned and varies according to the individuals concerned.

The risk reduction element of a sale or purchase involves removing some uncertainty, especially the possibility of discomfort, unpleasantness, failure or disaster, etc. We may buy a raincoat partially to avoid the unpleasantness of being wet, or we may buy a toothbrush to avoid the unpleasantness of bad breath or a visit to the dentist.

The service element of the sale or purchase has no effect on uncertainty and reflects more positive characteristics, such as the enhancement of value, enjoyment, self-esteem, reputation and comfort. Our raincoat may give us pleasure because it is comfortable to wear, because we feel it looks pleasant or because we enjoyed the way in which the transaction was handled at the shop where we purchased it.

Every successful selling/buying transaction brings both elements, risk reduction and service, to both parties. Each sale reduces the element of uncertainty on the part of the seller, he has got closer to recovering his investment, towards achieving his expected return. At the same time, each successful sale enhances his self-esteem, reputation, enjoyment, value and comfort. Similarly, each successful purchase has a similar but different effect on the purchaser. It will add to his enhancement of value, enjoyment, self-esteem, reputation and comfort and remove an element of uncertainty, fear or risk. It should be noted that we are not talking about fixed proportions. An individual product or service may have an overwhelming element of risk reduction and little element of service, as when one purchases a compulsory motor insurance from an unpleasant motor insurance salesman. Equally, the purchase of a product or service may have little risk reduction capability but may make us feel a lot better. This would certainly be true of a visit to the theatre or the cinema and would be true of many apparently risky activities, where, far from there being an apparent risk reduction, there is an increase of exposure to risk, which is, however, balanced by the enhancement. This would be the case with some of the more dangerous sports, where the enhancement of personal values outweights the apparent danger. Even in these cases, there is frequently an element of risk reduction. Although we increase our exposure to physical risk, we perhaps reduce the risk of social failure or failure of self-esteem.

So far we have been considering commercial risk and perhaps making the assumption that insurable risk has some essential differences. As we have seen, one difference that has been put forward by academics is that with insurable risk there is only the possibility of loss whereas with commercial risk, one has the possibility of loss or gain. Whilst the whole basis of insurance is the attempt to put the individual or company in the same financial position as if the loss had not occurred, this is difficult to achieve in practice. Once the vista is enlarged, it becomes perfectly possible to envisage a situation where gain results from the operation of an insurable event.

Insurers have always implicitly recognised this in their fear of "moral hazard", which must imply the possibility of gain from insurable events. Ignoring the possibly fraudulent intent implicit in moral hazard, we can think of many other situations where the operation of an insurable event followed by financial indemnity produces gain rather than loss. The mere fact of an insurance claim usually produces greater liquidity and hence greater flexibility. If this has been acquired at the expense of a missed opportunity, it will not be seen as an advantage, but if it has been acquired without any apparent disadvantage, then, the beneficiary is not just in a position of indemnity but distinctly better off than he was before the loss, when his cash was effectively locked up.

There has been a tendency in insurance literature to dwell too much on the negative aspects of the insurance purchase and the trade-off decision that this represents. While the purchase of insurance can be an unpleasant event, or can be induced merely by government regulation making the purchase of insurance compulsory, in practice most insurance transactions result in some enhancement of value, enjoyment, self-esteem, reputation and comfort. This can be seen as a feeling of security or comfort or wisdom that we have taken the right step in buying this insurance. It is also a feeling of confidence because we are insured; we feel that if this dreadful event occurs, we will receive financial recompense. Indeed, for some victims of accidents, insurance has an even greater role in shielding them from some of the more unpleasant consequences of the accident, as when an insurance company takes over the defence of a suit following a motor accident.

The whole subject of security, the feelings of the individual about security, the certainty of security and the uncertainty of his relationships with his fellow man, has been explored by Matthias Haller of the Graduate School of St. Gallen in Switzerland in a brilliant book "Sicherheit durch Versicherung?". This book, which is published with the aid of a substantial grant from a Swiss insurance company, is as yet, only available in German*. The title of the book "Security through Insurance?" and its subtitle "Thoughts on the Future Role of Insurance" indicate the subject, but the book contains a wealth of material showing the relationship between risk management and insurance from a personal and individual point of view as well as a company point of view.

From the point of view of risk management as a whole, this examination of insurance clearly shows that the dividing line between commercial and insurable risk is an imaginary one. It demonstrates the value of insurance in two elements of utility, risk reduction and service, and forces the view that insurance is no different in character from other goods and services which are bought and sold.

There has been a similar distinction, or rather an attempt to create a distinction between the treatment of the two types of risk on the part of insurance buyers and insurance academics. This has resulted in a tendency for risk management to be thought of in terms of insurable risk alone and in a parallel tendency for the management of insurable risk to become a specialised function within the company. This has tremendous dangers for any company in a time of rapid technological or social, political and environmental change.

The tendency towards separation of insurable and commercial risk, accompanied by specialisation in the treatment of insurable risk, has led to over-reliance on "hardware" to eliminate risk or the consequences of risk. In handling fire risk, for instance, this has meant over-reliance on sprinkler systems and automatic extinguishing devices which, instead of becoming a last line of defence, become, in many cases the first line. It is only a matter of time before a single line of defence that such systems present when given a unique role, becomes the target for the saboteur or the arsonist. This does not take account of the fact that even without any malevolent intent, constant emphasis on the efficiency of protective systems will dim the enthusiasm and ardour of one of the most effective risk control weapons, the human being.

---

* "Sicherheit durch Versicherung?" Matthias Haller, Bern, Herbert Lang, 1975.

There is a short paper in English on the same topic given by the author at a conference at Queen's College, Oxford in April 1976, and published in 'Papers in Risk Management 7 — The Oxford Conference' by Keith Shipton Developments Ltd., London.

Reasserting that risk is ubiquitous and comprehensive and that the handling of risk requires an overall approach, makes risk management more meaningful and more intelligible to top and line management. It reduces the tendency to leave it to the expert and makes possible the involvement of everyone in managing future uncertainty for the commercial and personal benefit of company and individual.

1.3 The Risk Management Process

Most, if not all, of the techniques used in risk management, are not new, but have been borrowed from other areas of commercial activity. What is new about risk management is the use of a method of integrating suitable techniques to identify, measure and manage threats. The typical risk management process is thus seen to consist of four main stages:

1. **The identification** or recognition of major threats to the company or organisation setting out to manage its risks. Some of these threats will be immediately obvious, others may be unseen or unrecognised.

2. Having successfully identified the major threats, the next stage is to **measure** those threats. By measurement we mean establishing how serious the threats are, in terms both of their potential severity or extent, and their probability of occurrence or relative frequency.

3. After recognition and measurement of the threats, the next stage is to prepare a plan for the **economic management** of those threats. This can include many techniques such as eliminating a particular activity because it is too dangerous, the use of protective measures, special training, special procedures and development of a risk management attitude.

4. The final stage after evolving a satisfactory risk management programme is to ensure that adequate **finance** is, or will be available to meet the impact of the potential threats that have been identified the first stage of the process. A variety of financing techniques are available, including insurance.

We can describe risk management as a formal planning method. As such it is similar to a number of other management techniques, including management by objectives, budgetary control and critical path analysis. Risk management is complementary to every one of these management techniques, and at the same time should be part of them. For example, the objectives set for management in Management by Objectives must include objectives in the field of managing risk. An effective budgetary control system must include controlling the cost of risk. Cost of risk can include insurance, all risk control measures, all uninsured losses and all other expenditure of finance risk. Critical path analysis must include analysing the threats and risks that will prevent the achievement of on-time budget performance which the system sets out to provide.

Chart 2 shows the essentials of risk management as a formal system for identification, measurement and control with recording and monitoring, to ensure that risk management is economic, i.e. that the results are worth more than the cost of providing them, and, defining responsibilities for risk management, so as to provide effective systems of defence.

RISK MANAGEMENT IMPLIES:

1. **A Formal System for**
   - Identifying/anticipating ⎫
   - Measuring ⎬ Threats
   - Controlling ⎭
   - Recording information and decisions
   - Monitoring results

2. **Economic Control**
   Adopting measures so that cost of control is less than financial benefits from
   - Reduced cost of loss
     and/or
   - Reduced probability of large loss

3. **Establishing Responsibilities** for Risk Management to provide effective defence against (larger) negative results of risk.

CHART 2—ESSENTIALS OF RISK MANAGEMENT

Chapter II

Risk Identification

2.1 The Risk Management Method

Chart 3 sets out an approach to introducing risk management into a company or organisation on a step-by-step basis.

---

1. CONSTRUCT RISK PROFILE
2. DETERMINE RISK OBJECTIVES
3. AUDIT EXISTING 'RISK MANAGEMENT'
4. PREPARE DETAILED PLANS & OBJECTIVES
5. TRAIN EXECUTIVES & MANAGERS
6. IMPROVE RISK MANAGEMENT CAPABILITY
7. MONITOR RISK MANAGEMENT PERFORMANCE

CHART 3—THE RISK MANAGEMENT METHOD

2.2 Risk Profile

The risk profile sets out to analyse the main risks facing the company and to understand its unique risk position whether in terms of its products, manufacturing methods, location, sales methods or the special skills of its management and workforce. When this profile is completed broad risk objectives usually in terms of risk control and risk financing can be determined.

Before preparing detailed plans for achieving these overall objectives, an audit of existing risk management, the practical measures by which local and central management actually handle the risk, will show the practicality of the overall objectives.

On completion of the detailed audit, new plans are prepared including training of executives and managers and the improvement of overall and local risk management capability.

The first part of this chapter covers the risk profile work and the second part describes the risk audit process. The following chapter on risk measurement shows how the material from risk profile and risk audit can be used to evaluate the risk prior to establishing risk control and financing objectives. Chapters IV and V cover the detailed objectives, training and improvement of capability for risk control and financing respectively.

Chapter VI describes the introduction of formal risk management into a company.

The first stage, called a general risk profile, is an attempt to state the unique risk characteristics and unique risk situation of a particular company or organisation at a particular time. It might start by examining the risks of the particular industry and move on to a more specific analysis of the particular company's or organisation's risk situation. Sources of information for such a risk profile include documents on the industry, company documents, and discussions with company executives and other staff.

This preliminary stage is intended to give a general understanding of the risk problems facing the company so that the major threats to the company's future earnings and prosperity can be identified.

Risk charts as shown in Charts 4, 5 and 6 can be used listing sources of risk, outlining the major assets exposed and making an assessment (which may only be provisional) of the extent of risks, particularly in terms of amounts exposed but also in terms of probability. These charts can be used in building up an analysis (Chart 7) of the major vulnerabilities of the company, as represented by the key activities or locations (such as individual workshops) on which a substantial part of the company's ultimate profit depends. Particular parts of the organisation may not, on their own, account for a major part of the earnings, but the subsequent achievement by other parts of the business or high earnings may be dependent upon the activities that are concentrated there, and they can thus be identified as a major vulnerability.

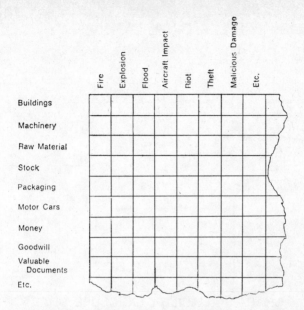

CHART 4—PROPERTY EXPOSURE CHART

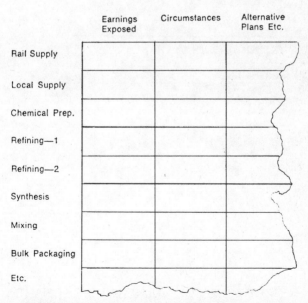

CHART 5—EARNINGS EXPOSURE CHART

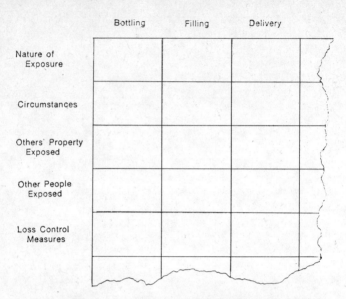

CHART 6—LIABILITY EXPOSURE CHART

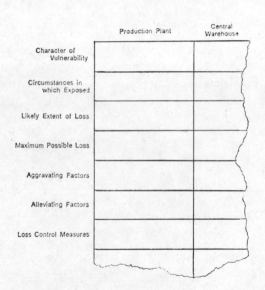

CHART 7—MAJOR VULNERABILITY CHART

Column 2 again shows the sources of such information.

As well as company documents and discussions with key officials, site visits may be required to locate and identify particular risk characteristics. For this work, use of non-company technical data will probably be essential. This could include information on particular types of machinery, including its replacement time, the different chemicals used in processes or other key risk information.

It will inevitably be necessary to consider check lists. These can prove invaluable to the person seeking to establish the problem areas in a business, but a word of warning is necessary. Whilst check lists are essential to ensure that the basic criteria are not overlooked, one is always dealing with a rapidly changing situation and any check list prepared yesterday may now be out of date. In identifying risk, therefore, one needs to use a number of alternative checks, to use intuition and to ensure that any identification is checked carefully by others, particularly by those who are involved in the day to day process that is under examination.

2.3 Types of Threats

Looking first at the major threats that face most companies we can break them down into the following types:

1) **Physical Threats**

   Physical threats include injury and death and all forms of loss or damage to property. The causes of physical loss will usually be common perils, such as fire, explosion, flood, earthquake, physical collision, pollution, contamination, lightning but it may also result from arson, theft, vandalism, rioting, or deterioration of property and damage or loss caused by human error.

2) **Liability Risks**

   Liabilities can be divided into claims from customers of the business, from employees of the business and from the public generally. Whilst liability claims can result from the factors mentioned under physical threats, one must also consider claims which are related to the product or services provided by the company, the effects of contractual liability to customers, suppliers or others and the effect of national and international regulations and laws. The latter can be quite onerous for companies, particularly in the light of the vast awards made by some courts in the United States of America and elsewhere.

3) **Business Interruption**

Losses of this kind will follow the physical threats and liabilities already considered. Here it is necessary to consider the effect of the potential loss on the company's production processes on other operations, including such factors as reliance on suppliers, supplies to suppliers, particular reliance on records and systems, especially where computers are employed, and also the political and social consequences of, for example, the enforced closure of processing plants because of pollution. Other threats include loss of market or goodwill, and industrial action.

4) **Loss of Materials and Resources**

These threats affect the resources or materials essential to the processing of the company's products and include for example paper shortages in a service industry, national and local supplies of energy and labour resources. The origins of these threats will to some extent overlap with those already considered, but in the case of energy, for example, could include the effect of an increase in fuel prices on products in the world market.

5) **Social Risks**

The effect of social change on the company is a growing threat and this category includes changes in habit, the consequences of unemployment, delinquency, large city financial difficulties, and increases in vandalism, arson and theft.

6) **Political Risks**

We have considered apart from the effects of political change mentioned under the heading of Business Interruption loss of materials and resources but additional problems include new legislation, consumerism, the effects of inflation and specific legislative difficulties, for example, the sudden imposition of import controls.

7) **Environmental Risks**

Identification of environmental risks implies recognition of existing environmental changes and some anticipation of likely future changes. One would need to take into account the effects of climate, such as the unexpected drought in 1976. The factors to be assessed would include depreciation in resources, consideration of alternative supplies, which might result in increased cost, and the possible necessity of changing technology.

8) **Management Risk**

Poor management can have a major effect on companies, although the cost may often be hidden until the results of poor management show themselves as particular events which have a significant effect on the company's fortunes. Examples of management threats are wastage, including poor packaging, poor stock control, and corrosion, poor planning control and poor staff selection. Examples of poor planning might include the inability of the company to keep up to date with technological change resulting in a reduced demand for its products and services, and inadequate product development capabilities resulting in product failure and subsequent loss of market.

The majority of the threats outlined above can be identified and managed. It is certainly possible to argue that physical threats, liability risks, business interruption and technological change can be directly managed by a company but that social risks, political risks, environmental risks, loss of materials and other resources while potentially controllable are not capable of direct influence in some cases. It is still possible, however, to identify and anticipate the consequences of these threats and to take action to reduce the company's vulnerability in the areas of greatest concern. This action may be justified to transfer the risk where appropriate or even to eliminate it directly by, for example, stopping production in countries where the risk of earthquake is considered to present a far greater potential risk than can be justified the profits involved or the social reasons for staying in those countries.

Before we consider methods of identifying threats in greater detail, it will be helpful to consider the basic purposes of identification which are:

1)   To acquire information about types and causes of losses including potential areas for loss of production.

2)   To build up knowledge of the company's business and operating philosophy.

3)   To determine the frequency and classification of the risks identified.

4)   To determine the need for loss financing.

Many writers in the past have commented upon the difficulty of risk identification. This difficulty is increased by the need to keep the search within the bounds of economy of cost and the acceptability of the search methods used for top and operating management.

Whilst risk identification is considered here as a separate activity, it is not possible in practice to separate it from the measurement of risk and from loss control. The charts in the appendix will also be helpful for controlling and financing risk.

2.4   External Sources of Information

It is desirable during the risk identification process to look outside the company to check information obtained during internal discussions and site visits. Wider information can usually be obtained about the industry in which the company operates in order to balance the information collected with similar situations elsewhere and also to locate specialist sources which can add something to the information derived from internal source discussions. These external sources can include suppliers to the company, suppliers to those suppliers, competitors, distributors, distributors to distributors, government sources, especially concerning existing and potential legislation, published information from the industry, customers, especially key customers on whom there is particular financial reliance, and a number of outside advisers, who may include insurance companies, loss control consultants, and financial and legal advisers.

Examples of external information sources would include stock market material, including stockbrokers' reports on the company, material about the industry, including information about the financial accounts of competitors, major events in the industry, technological developments and changes. Government reports on the company and the industry, if any are available, will be useful. Advertising used both by the company and its competitors may give clues to vulnerabilities and examination of market research studies may help. All these examinations need to be carried out wherever the company operates. Much of the source material can be obtained by local management and transmitted to the person carrying out the risk identification.

2.5 Internal Sources of Information

Sources of information can be divided into internal and external.

Internal sources cover operational management, including representatives at central offices and local level, functional departments, especially financial, administrative, personnel and marketing. The search will probably be conducted by a combination of meetings, group discussions, and detailed individual examination of the company's records, reports, site plans, management systems etc. These discussions and examinations will be supported by site visits to both offices and production sections of the company as appropriate.

Examination of records will normally include a detailed analysis of the company's annual report and accounts, studying the basic activities of the company and evaluating the relative importance of these individual activities to the company's overall performance, in order to highlight particular areas of potential vulnerability. Analysis of the turnover and pre-tax profit figures will show the size of the company and its performance in relation to its competitors, to its own previous year's performance and, read in conjunction with the statement by the Board, to future trends.

Reports and accounts also give indications of the management structure of the company, its involvement in other companies and its geographical spread, both within single countries and world wide. They may also give indications of vulnerability in particular areas and help to build a broad picture of the company, its prosperity and its vulnerabilities, whether commercial, political and social.

An examination of the information distributed internally by the company will give a general indication of its attitude socially both to employees and customers. House magazines can give more information about the management structure outlined in the annual reports and may also give some indication of future developments within the company both managerially and in relation to products or services.

The interviews with central office and local operating management are also designed at this stage to provide a broad background to the company and its activities.

Discussions with the Chairman or Chief Executive of the company may cover the future plans of the company, its management style in terms of autonomy, central control and the role of head office. Other factors would include the history of the company, its particular problem areas and the Chief Executive's own view of the major existing and future threats he foresees both in relation to the company's existing, and its planned activities.

Discussions with financial executives would include an analysis of the management accounting systems, the importance both in turnover and profit terms of each product, location and country. The company's attitude to risk taking, risk evaluation and use of insurance and self-insurance methods would be considered, together with the methods by which the company budgeted both for current and projected expenditure. The extent of the company's current and future borrowing requirements and the types of financing used would be important as would the advisability of the company carrying insurance deductibles in view of the degree of acceptance of financial risk taking. Detailed discussions of the risk carried within the financial areas of the company may be held, including analysis of the internal audit system, the dependency of the company on computer installations; both internal and external, and the systems used for protection of records.

Discussions with central office production management can include an outline of the purpose and significance of the premises and of individual products or services, leading to identification of key areas in turnover and profit terms, so that a programme of risk identification site visits could be drawn up. A broad definition of the operational methods used would be needed, including job descriptions, spheres of responsibility, codes of practice, and the general attitude to safety.

Further discussions would need to be held about the reliance of the company on particular suppliers, the availability of alternative sources, the use of buffer stocks, the seasonality of the business and all the problems connected with dependency on others. Similar questions need to be asked in respect of any key machinery or employees on whom the company rely, to identify potential bottlenecks in its operations. The company's policy in relation to spares and stock control, availability of outside maintenance staff, alternative suppliers of machines, service dependencies would also need to be checked.

The marketing department of the company will probably be able to gauge the effect of loss of production on the company's goodwill and its market, the position in relation to competitors and whether help from competitors is a possible solution to the problems raised by an emergency.

These discussions, will also encompass the extent to which loss control can be built in as part of the Company's management philosophy or structure. Questions concerning loss control include whether the company employs loss control specialists, and if so, whether they have line or functional responsibilities, the lines of reporting and communication of incidents, the level at which line management have loss control responsibility, whether the company has a formal method of monitoring its loss control, the effects of legislation, and whether the incidents which have occurred within the company can be monitored by comparing them with similar situations elsewhere in the industry or at other locations of the company.

2.6 Risk Audit and Check Lists

Although there is no hard and fast division between information needed in risk profile and risk audit, most of this chapter so far has been concerned with the main external and internal sources of information for risk profile work. We now move on to the more detailed phase, usually linked with risk audit.

Before moving on to more detailed checklists and methods of charting we can tabulate the particular types of risks that we have considered, splitting them into three areas of analysis (Charts 8, 9 and 10):

Analysis by source
- natural hazard
- man-affected natural hazard
- man-made accidental
- man-made deliberate
- social and political
- progressive deterioration
- wrong judgment

CHART 8—ANALYSIS BY SOURCE

Analysis by area of operation
— internal
— external
— natural environment
— social environment
— localised geographically
— localised socially
— supplier chain
— customer chain

CHART 9—ANALYSIS BY AREA OF OPERATION

Analysis by effect
ON PEOPLE
— employees
— public
— customers
ON PROPERTY
— own property
— other property
ON EARNINGS
— consequent on other types of loss or damage
— economic loss
— social and market conditions
— speculative
— currency
— commodities

CHART 10—ANALYSIS BY EFFECT

The Appendix includes detailed checklists covering the following areas:

Risk financing and insurance
Site tours
Administration

Transport and fork-lift truck operations

Marketing

Personnel

Computer

Employee safety

Legal

Property

Product development and quality control

Fire and security

Purchasing

Engineering

Emergency planning

These lists overlap as they are designed as questionnaires for use with different sections of company management. This overlap however will help to check the answers from people representing different points of view and will enable the investigator to check the answers to his enquiries from many different angles. Check lists for risk identification work should be regarded as clues which help to indicate subjects and areas which will help to open up the discussions and provide a detailed analysis of the threats facing both individual parts of the company being investigated and the company overall. They will need to be recorded carefully as they will form the basis for the detailed analytical work which will take place later. The basic lists provided in the Appendix can be broadened as a result of the initial discussions at Head Office of the company in order to relate them more specifically to the operations of the company concerned eliminating irrelevant areas and ensuring that the whole spectrum of the company's activities is included.

It will probably be helpful to start discussions by the use of the general list which is included in this chapter. It will provide the basis on which subsequent individual check lists can be adapted or developed depending on the requirements of the study and the particular areas that will need close investigation.

2.7 General Checklist

The first questions are:—

What is the business?

What types of products or services is the company involved in?

Are they unique?

Are they part of established technology?

What are their future prospects and what are the likely social, political and economic factors that could influence their future development?

It will be necessary not only to consider the existing business in its many forms but any future plans for diversification or contraction both in respect of products and expansion into other markets and countries.

As a consequence the type of plant or process involved in the various areas of the company's operations will be renewed:—

Whether these are common or unique?

What the origins are of the plant?

The ages of the machinery and factories involved?

Historical and possible future changes?

Having considered the Company's business and the processes by which it produces its products or services its customers, it will be necessary to consider:—

Who are the existing customers?

Who are the competitors?

What are the levels of revenue both on a general and individual customer basis and the respective gross profits?

Sales will be split into home and exports, with information on the territories involved and the proportion of revenue derived from each territory and each product. Other **customer-related** factors include any seasonal features of the business and analysis of key customers and information on the exposures likely to arise from individual customer relationships, and the effect of any losses both as a percentage of existing and future revenue.

Other sales factors include any major dependencies on regional sales operations, and income in the form of services or royalties.

The **marketing operations** will be considered in relation to the effect on the market if the product could not be manufactured. Information for each particular product on the lead-time available in respect of finished goods, distributors' stocks, customers' stocks and possible availability from elsewhere in the group or from outside. For rebuilding, this will be related, in time comparison terms, to the availability factors or possibly the timing of relocation if using other available premises either inside or outside the group. Other factors considered will include possible assistance from competitors, foreign producers and the possibilities of the development of contingency planning techniques if these are not already being used within the operations.

The **processing and production** factors within the company take into account the raw materials on which the operation is dependent, the range of raw materials involved and the major items, the possible difficulties and shortages both in respect of future reduction in supply, and possible political problems in respect of raw materials imported from overseas. Specific information will be needed about items where the sudden loss of supply would be serious and where there is no alternative or complete replacement available in the short term.

These areas can be quantified in terms of what the effect would be, what are the alleviating factors in terms of stock-piles, spread of supply of sites, alternative materials, alternative foreign suppliers, competitor aid etc. The discussions will investigate ways in which these risks can be reduced, perhaps by multiple-sourcing, contingency planning as mentioned above, or inspection of key supplier and distributor sites.

If multiple-sourcing is already practised by the company, the basic policy and the methods of monitoring for problems will be discussed. The effects of stockpile loss will be related to the use of stocks contained in one building, monitoring of the loss control methods, and the individual effect, in particular buildings, of stock loss, split into type of product, raw materials and other relevant factors.

It will also be necessary to investigate what energy and other consumables the company operations depend on. These can be split into power, fuel, water, gas, steam and other areas.

The investigation into dependence on **power** will examine the sources, the feeders, the importance of the power to the company's operation and the aspects of protection. **Fuels** will investigate the nature, sources, the methods of transport, the available stocks, the effect of stock loss and, once again, their importance to the operations and similarly in relation to **water, gas and steam.** In the category of **other energy and consumable dependencies,** the areas include packaging, catalysts, electrodes, solvent and treatment materials. It will be necessary to split these between sources within the company and sources outside.

The dependencies of the company in its production processes will be considered in greater detail including factors such as problems in obtaining spares, the existing spares holding system, the key items, the monitored lead-time on high turnover spares, location of spares stocks and vulnerabilities if they are in a single location, and also whether, they are split by types of spares, and whether it is possible for these systems to be changed in order to avoid too much reliance on one area.

In the area of **transport,** information will be required on the use of vehicles and their importance to the company, whether they are owned by the company, whether there are any specially—or purpose-built vehicles, the possible exposure from accumulation of vehicles on one site, and the use by contractors and other outside companies of vehicles on the company's own premises. Other more general areas of transport include methods used, for example, whether products or raw materials are transported within or outside the country by sea, what products are involved, what are the alternative docks, and what are the particular problems in relation to importing or exporting to particular countries. Similar questions will be answered in respect of rail, road, pipelines and other transport methods. Special attention needs to be paid to whether or not special ships, cranes, aircraft, or railcars are necessary and what would be the availability of these special vehicles in the event of one or a number of them being destroyed.

Other general dependencies include sub-processes, both outside and inside the company, laboratories, computers, including process computers, telephones, key external storage facilities or services, patterns or moulds, patents and trade marks.

In the **organisational and personnel** areas it will be necessary to obtain a detailed organisation structure, information on the key personnel, the status of risk management within the company in respect of insurance, fire, security, employee safety, records, the methods of management, and whether it is autonomous divisionally or within particular countries. Other personnel factors include the characteristics of the work force, the methods of payment of wages, turnover problems, absenteeism, industrial action, work force shortages, travel and exposures of key personnel.

It will be necessary to investigate **general threats** to resources including such factors as flood, water leakage, aircraft, storm, lightning, subsidence, activities of neighbours, disease, ransom and consequential damage to systems and processes. At the appropriate level in the company arson, sabotage, riot, breakdown and employee safety aspects will be discussed.

2.8 Charting Risk Exposures

The charting of exposures resulting from the detailed identification work can be done in a number of ways depending on the needs of the particular investigation.   Four examples of charting are now considered with examples of the layouts used.

The first example (Chart 11) is a simple method which shows only the risk situation identified during the search with a broad recommendation for diminishing or eliminating the risk. The examples used in the chart are the result of a broad site visit, which was designed to obtain the overview of the major threats facing the company, but to mention any obvious areas for immediate attention where these were recognised. This method of charting would not be used for any quantification of the risk, but merely to provide a useful format for recording the areas identified.

This charting method can be expanded, if desired, by listing the threats to the organisation, the exposure to risk in specific terms, an estimate of the potential loss in terms of severity and recommendations for loss control.

The next example (Chart 12) goes further by giving more detailed information concerning loss control under the headings of exposure, sources of risk, possible loss severity, and the alleviating and the aggravating factors. This charting method is a useful one when carrying out a major risk management investigation, as it has the advantage of starting with the major threats to the company, broken down logically into the various sources, and then dealing with quantification of the exposure and possible methods of control.

The problems of estimating the severity of losses will be dealt with in greater detail in the following chapter on risk measurement.

It is hoped that the impression has not been given that

RISK SITUATIONS	RECOMMENDATIONS
1. Security	
(a) Nearby factory warehouses containing potentially hazardous materials.	More detailed knowledge and research is required before risk assessment.
(b) Inadequate security arrangements regarding the quota of security personnel to perform their functions effectively.	Employ a system of visual monitoring of personnel movements and premises.
(c) Important documentary information, including tickets.	Improve the efficiency of the existing strongroom and consolidate the arrangements for fireproof storage.
(d) Transfer of cash by the company's own personnel.	Develop safer transfer routes to minimise risk to individuals e.g. travel with more than one person varying the route. Consult the advice of safety contractors.
(e) Misplacement of tickets.	Transfer to a safe mode of storage.
2. Liability	
(a) Flexes from domestic appliances leading to dangerous situations in public access areas.	Remove hazard, clear access routes.
(b) Unguarded guillotine machine.	Attach an adequate guard to protect all access to the danger area.
(c) Dangerous access to toxic cleaning chemicals by employees.	Keep all dangerous chemicals locked away with key availability controlled.
3. Fire	
(a) Fire extinguisher label dated and inaccurate in description.	Institute regular maintenance and inspection systems to ensure no repetition in future.
(b) Fire risks in many offices caused by portable electric appliances attached to long unwieldy flexes, located near stationery.	Securely amount appliances in a permanent location. Store office stationery in a safe place.
(c) Inadequate storage of waste materials and flammables: present system involves storage with stationery supplies.	Institute a new system of waste disposal, including chemical segregation and special treatment of toxic and flammable substances. Employ a suitable recording system for all hazardous material disposed.

CHART 11—RISK IDENTIFIED AND RECOMMENDATIONS

EXPOSURE	SOURCES	POSSIBLE LOSS SEVERITY	ALLEVIATING FACTORS	AGGRAVATING FACTORS
(a) Operations discontinuing involving several associated companies.	Disruptions including:— — energy/mechanical supplies; — energy propellants for plant operations; — British Rail transport system; — port and shipping restrictions; — road transport.	Profit declination if the disruption is prolonged.	Generally stable employer/employee relationship.	Inadequacy by some middle management personnel in understanding labour grievances. Middle management may require a greater degree of training to combat situations effectively.
(b) Misplacement of valuable information and documents.	EDP documents by contingent fires, flooding, sabotage, misappropriation. Industrial espionage. Fraud. Forgery. Ownership record.	Certain costs are accrued when a major reinstatement of information is needed. Possible operations disruption, according to the nature of the records lost.	Awareness of contingency dangers due to:— intimidation of security systems; fire in strongroom or sale; sophisticated auditings; check system on securities and business checks.	Time-lag before fraud or sabotage events are discovered. Need for a microfilm security system to allow rapid reconstruction of details and plans after loss. Lengthy legal entanglements.
(c) Liability due to professional erratum and negligence.	Consulting engineers and technologists. Projects for third parties including design and scale of systems: — designers/planners; — quantity surveyors.	Could be of considerable magnitude if "client" suffers interruption to his business.	The quality and magnitude of experience the company has acquired in all areas where it undertakes consultancy work.	Need for the participation of formal exposure estimates as an added part of project consultancy work. A monetary limitation of liability is advisable where there is any abnormal degree of exposure or not, or when the loss potential may be greater than the company's current liability insurance level.
(d) Contingent major fire occurring in the head office.	— accidental; — arson; — sabotage.	Additional costs incurred:— — major repair; — extra working costs accrued by displacement of administrative work; — loss of information and valuable records; — employee injury resulting in compensation payments and similar indemnities owed by the company.	Information and record presenting systems:— — organised fire drills and emergency plans; — lowrise buildings preferable; — security patrols of premises after working hours.	Tighter security/visitor controls. Protection of key areas by small detection systems. Employment of a contingency plan to isolate the main problem areas and create preventative measures against fire and other physical disturbances.

CHART 12—A MORE DETAILED RISK CHART

the risk identification process should be carried out solely by a risk manager, insurance company loss control representative, safety officer, consultant, or indeed by any one person on his own. The essence of the process is to involve as many people within the company as possible in discussions of the major threats to the operations of their own area of activity. In many instances, companies have delegated the risk identification process to operating managers, using a risk management advisory function as a support activity where needed, and also to co-ordinate the results of the overall identification process. In this way local management is able to concentrate on the area of its own responsibility, using detailed questionnaires provided by the risk management function, which enable them to develop the necessary broad view of the problem, and at the same time encourage a practical approach to methods of loss reduction.

In one particular example the brief given to the individual operating unit was to identify the company's main risk or exposures to accidental loss involved in its area of operation, with the aim of providing an aid to management in the recognition and establishment of priorities in overall risk management planning effort and expenditure. This prime objective was supported by a secondary target of reviewing the current effort within the unit to reduce risk, and recommending further measures for risk prevention considered to be practical. In order to prevent the surveys from becoming unreliable because of over-familiarity with the existing system, the effort of the local management was supplemented by adding to the identification team a member of local management in another unit of the company's operations. This approach, together with the support and guidance of the risk management function, provided the right mix of local responsibility and monitoring control, particularly in relation to the evaluation of potential losses, which needed to have some common denominator within the company overall for them to have any real value as a basis for central decision.

Chapter III

Risk Measurement

3.1 Measurement of Risk

Although risk measurement is presented in this book as a separate topic it should not be seen as a self-contained separate activity. Risk identification and measurement are together evaluation of risk. The main reason for both activities is to provide assistance in practical decision taking about risk. After considering the risk as evaluated we may decide not to go ahead with the project or to continue the activity subject to the adoption of risk control measures.

There are many reasons for risk measurement and the most important are shown in Chart 13. The time and effort to be spent on risk measurement must be related to the value of the data. It may be easy to establish that we cannot accept a certain risk, but more difficult to determine the after-loss replacement value for insurance of a large factory.

We will need to estimate how much it will cost to build a new factory after allowing for such factors as site clearance and the need to conform to new building regulations. The machinery may be of foreign manufacture so that we have to consider the delivery time, changes in price and change in exchange value. It will be seen that there is an overlap between risk measurement and risk financing. Looked at narrowly risk measurement is concerned with the values exposed, the probability of loss and the likely or possible severity of loss whereas risk financing is concerned with the likely post-loss financing need and methods of meeting it.

If we equate risk with uncertainty as suggested in Chapter I how can we measure that uncertainty? There seems to be a contradiction in the very concept of measuring uncertainty, in the sense that if one could measure it, there would not be uncertainty.

REASONS FOR RISK MEASUREMENT

1. COMMERCIAL RISK DECISIONS
   — is the risk too big in relation to the return?
   — is there too much uncertainty for us to handle?

2. LOSS CONTROL DECISIONS
   — how can the risk be controlled?
   — how much will it cost to control it?
   — how will this loss control activity affect the expected cost of loss?

3. RISK FINANCING DECISIONS
   — how much will (could) losses cost?
   — how can we finance likely and possible losses?
   — (for insurable risks) how does the cost of insurance compare with our estimate of likely or possible risk cost?
   — how much insurance do we need? (value insured, cover limit or liability limit).

CHART 13—REASONS FOR RISK MEASUREMENT

In Chapter II we have covered the identification of risk or the determination of which risks our enterprise is exposed to and in what circumstances. In risk measurement we attempt to measure the probability of a risk event happening and the likely loss that will result.

3.2 Risk Frequency

The probability of a risk event can be described as its frequency of occurrence. If it is an event that happens several or many times a year such as the occurrence of rainfall or the involvement of one of a large fleet of motor vehicles in a road accident we will have available statistics that enable us to form a view of future likely frequency with some confidence.

In both cases we can take a view of the likelihood of occurrence but it is in fact very unlikely that the actual result over a period of a year will coincide with our estimate. Past experience may show over say ten years that the average number of rainy days was 127 but the number in any particular year has ranged between 96 and 181. 127 days represents a reasonable expectation but we know from past experience that the number of rainy days could be anywhere between 96 and 181. The possible range is in fact much higher—if we want to be safe we should say that the range is between 0 and 365 (or 366 if a leap year).

In this particular case we are likely to have more information available in that we will probably know the actual number of days for each of the ten years. Perhaps the range is either of the following cases:—

	131	96	142	131	121	181	110	112	130	114
or	96	111	109	106	142	143	109	135	140	181

In the first case it looks as though both 96 and 181 are extreme cases but without them there is still a spread between 110 and 142. The last four years show an average of 116 which could either suggest a change in the weather or that a more rainy spell is due. In the second case we have the problem that the first year is 96 and the last year is 181. The average for the first four years is 103 and that for the last four years is 150, perhaps (but only perhaps) suggesting that the weather is getting more rainy. How confident would you feel in each case about next year's rainfall?

Looking at the problem of motor accidents in a large fleet we might have a similar pattern but could logically draw more confident conclusions from them. Using the same figures we could perhaps assume an improving safety trend in the first set of figures and a sharp deterioration in the second set of figures even though the overall result is very similar.

3.3 Statistical Correction

There are various practical difficulties in analysing several years' loss records, especially as we are often as concerned with cost (severity) of accidents as the number (frequency) of accidents.

In some cases we can make allowances for the factors as for:—

1.   Number of vehicles—we need to relate the accident rate to the number of vehicles (and other factors) to determine whether our loss experience is getting better and to assess future cost.

2.   Inflation—the cost of vehicle accidents will obviously rise if prices rise. We need to make a correction for this both in assessing performance and estimating future cost.

To put several years' figures on a common basis for number of units (vehicles) at risk and inflation we need to correct for both factors. We might consider two sets of figures, the fleet size and an index for repair costs if we were concerned with accidental damage (the index for liability costs would be different).

For units exposed we can put a previous year's figures on a comparable basis by the formula:

$$\frac{\text{CURRENT YEAR FLEET}}{\substack{\text{STATISTICAL YEAR}\\\text{UNDER CONSIDERATION}}} \quad \times \quad \substack{\text{STATISTICAL YEAR}\\\text{NUMBER OF}\\\text{ACCIDENTS}}$$

To bring a past year's accidental cost up to date we would use a similar formula:

$$\frac{\text{CURRENT INDEX}}{\substack{\text{INDEX FOR}\\\text{STATISTICAL YEAR}\\\text{UNDER CONSIDERATION}}} \quad \times \quad \substack{\text{STATISTICAL YEAR}\\\text{ACCIDENT COST}}$$

These two corrections are very useful in bringing our loss experience up to date but for a vehicle fleet there are many other factors that could affect our loss record including:—

1.   Number of vehicle miles—if miles per vehicle year remain constant we can discount this factor.

2.   Vehicle density—although analysis of national road traffic figures shows that there is not a direct co-relation.

3.   Road changes—there is a relationship between type of road and accident per vehicle mile. Motorways have less accidents per vehicle mile but the accidents are more serious.

4. Weather—a variation in number of icy and foggy days will directly affect number of accidents.

5. Changes in road traffic law and road traffic enforcement.

6. Changes in driver selection, training and experience.

The list is not exclusive and our ability to take each factor into account varies. It is worth trying to do this but the basis of calculation should be recorded and critically reviewed in the light of experience.

3.4 Severity of Risk

Earlier in this chapter we referred to the two main dimensions of risk management as the probability of a risk event or its frequency and the seriousness of a risk event which we will call **severity.**

The severity of a risk event depends on the value exposed to risk and the degree of damage. The value exposed in a risk event has several components:—

1. The value of the property at risk

2. Any additional expenses that would or could result from the risk event

3. Loss of earnings due to non-availability of productive assets

4. Any damage or injury to third parties and others that could result in further financial loss.

It will be seen that there can be a loss exceeding 100% of the nominal value exposed. If we examine the financial loss in terms of the post-loss financing cost of replacement we may find many factors that would further increase the loss. A serious explosion involving loss of life may mean that rebuilding is delayed pending the completion of official enquiries. Public protest or local government regulation may prevent rebuilding on the existing site, thus causing further delay and cost.

Looking at risk in terms of insurable risk rather than commercial risk we can recognise the division of risk into three different types of insurance:—

1. Property insurance will cover the value of the property at risk and it is usually possible to extend the insurance to cover additional expenses

2. Consequential loss insurance will cover loss of earnings due to an insured event

3. Liability insurance will give financial protection against liability suits for damage or injury.

Most of the techniques used to calculate insured value and cover limits required are useful for risk measurement but we are also concerned with various loss situations, including the probability of partial loss. Our evaluation of all loss possibilities from small losses up to catastrophic total loss will enable us to decide on the right balance of loss control, self-insurance and insurance.

3.5 Relationship between Frequency and Severity

So far we have looked separately at frequency (probability of occurrence) and severity (size of loss) of risk events. In practice there is a close relationship between them. We can expect that small losses will be much more frequent than large losses but this relationship need not be a linear one.

Talking generally we could consider losses in the form of a pyramid:

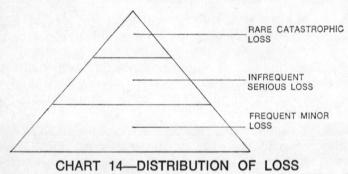

CHART 14—DISTRIBUTION OF LOSS

In this pyramid, total loss of the asset or unit concerned is at the top, serious damage at the middle and frequent loss at the base. We could, if statistics were available, relate the areas concerned to the loss potential but the limited data we have suggests different pyramids for different classes of risk. For ships in general about 30% would be in the top sector, for aircraft more than 50%, for motor vehicles a typical figure would be 30%—40% for a very large factory perhaps as little as 15% (on an industry wide basis) but for smaller factories a much larger percentage. The division in each case between the second and third category would be dependent on the values chosen.

Where figures are available we can plot in graph form

the probability (number of events) against the severity (size of loss) to give us a loss curve.

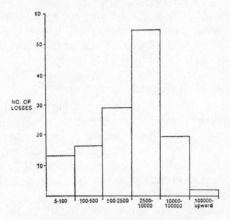

CHART 15—SIZE OF LOSS

NOTE—there is no relationship between area and total cost of loss.

Taking this chart we can convert the plotted figures into a loss curve as follows:—

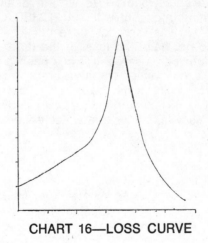

CHART 16—LOSS CURVE

When sufficient reliable data is available, the use of statistical techniques may be valuable. Either by plotting results on a graph or by mathematical calculation, the statistician can tell us a great deal about the probable pattern of results, especially the scatter of likely results.

(A knowledge of statistical techniques is recommended for the risk management adviser but is outside the scope of this book in which we have avoided repetition of generally available material from other disciplines).

3.6   Limitation of Statistical Techniques

Most textbooks and courses on risk management contain sections describing statistical techniques and recommending their use. However we have found considerable danger in practice on over-reliance on statistical techniques.   The biggest danger concerns the large unexpected loss, although problems have arisen with sharp deterioration in loss experience through small-losses.

This illustrates one of the most difficult problems in risk management. We can usually evaluate with reasonable accuracy and confidence the pattern and overall cost of small losses enabling us to plan economic risk control. We use the term economic to show a situation where the cost of losses saved (measured in terms of reduced losses following introduction of risk control) is much greater than the cost of loss control.

For the large catastrophic loss we are dealing not with a frequency distribution but with an EITHER/OR situation. We may have the loss in which case our loss control has failed or we do not have the loss. In the latter case we do not know whether our loss control has been a major factor or not. There is no convenient measure of economic loss control. The probability of the catastrophic loss may be estimated at say 1 in 50,000 with the cost of the disaster at say £42 million. This would give an expected cost of loss of

$$42,000,000 \times \frac{1}{50,000} = £840.$$

The problem is what confidence can we place in our estimated probability of 1 in 50,000? For an insurer with say 1,000 similar risks there is sufficient frequency to form a statistical population in turn giving a basis for our calculation.

In practice the decision on what to spend on catastrophic loss prevention must be a subjective one. As we shall see in the next chapter the decision is assisted by various factors, including health and safety and other legislation which require certain steps to be taken.

We strongly recommend that the risk management adviser starts his work on risk measurement from consideration of the worst possible situation and only takes into account loss control measures that reduce that loss potential with certainty. This will ensure that the possibility of catastrophic loss is borne in mind by management at all times and all reasonable action taken. One of the dangers of calculation of very low probability serious loss is to create a feeling that this is an acceptable risk and that the risk is managed.

RISK MEASUREMENT GUIDELINES

1. Risk measurement is difficult but we improve with practice and feedback.

2. Therefore we should keep full records of our calculations so that we can check predictions against actual results and account for any differences.

3. Similarly we should state our basic assumptions and make sure that all decision-makers understand them.

4. One must not try to make the facts fit the theory. If our calculations disagree with actual results—we are wrong. Therefore we should study the differences to help us get it right next time.

CHART 17—RISK MEASUREMENT GUIDELINES

In Charts 18 and 19 will be found some practical questions for help in measuring risk.

3.7 Statistical Data

Most risk measurement situations deal with situations for which a great deal of data is available. The situation may be specific and relate to our company only or it may be a general situation. In both cases we need to assess the differences:—

1. Between our situation and the situation(s) for which data is available

2. Between the historic situation recorded in the data and the likely course of events over the future period we are considering.

FREQUENCY

There is a relationship between frequency and severity.

1. **Small Regular loss**
   — sufficient size of sample needed
   — we can then say — if the world doesn't change
   this will **probably** happen

To measure the future we need to know:—
   — size of error if no change
   — areas of possible change
   — extent of possible change

2. **Medium Irregular Loss**
   — what **could** happen?
   — how often?
   — what can we do about it?

3. **Large Very Rare Loss**
   — what would happen
   — how much could it cost
   — how will we finance it?

CHART 18

This shows risk measurement as having two vital components. The first is critical analysis of available statistics.

Who collected the statistics?

How were they recorded?

Is there any bias in the collection or recording?

What assumptions were made in classifying the data?

How do our circumstances differ from those reflected in the statistics—technical and personal?

The second component is analysing the future course of events. Some guidance is available from trends that are discernible in the present (statistical and otherwise). Many others can be deduced from knowledge of today's events.

To give an illustration. If we continue to increase automation we will probably increase vulnerability in terms of dependence on more complex, more concentrated areas of production with less people available to put it right. Similarly the engineers who maintain that equipment will have greater bargaining power. We might get increased opposition to automation as employment shrinks.

At first sight the problem is a difficult if not impossible one. In practice there are only two main alternatives. To ignore the future or to try and manage it. We have greater chance of success if we try and manage it. This requires a straightforward approach of recognising that we cannot get it right every time so that some mistakes are inevitable. However if we recognise after the event that we did not make the right analysis we can learn and improve our skills in tackling other future problems. Therefore we should record all our assumptions and calculations not as an alibi but an aid to better work.

In Chart 19 we show some questions for work with loss experience statistics.

LOSS EXPERIENCE STATISTICS

Review available statistics
- — for this operation/company
- — for this industry
- — for this country
- — international

Are these statistics relevant?

How do our circumstances differ?
- — time
- — place
- — processes/operations
- — management
- — loss control measures
- — staff/employees
- — volume sales/units

Can we correct?

adjust for   —   volume
- — inflation
- — special circumstances (subjective)

CHART 19

IMPORTANT WARNING

All statistics include basic assumptions.
Make sure you know and understand them—read the foot-notes.
When using different sources bring them to a common basis — and state your assumptions.

3.8 Property Risk Management

From Chart 13 we established the reasons for risk measurement as making risk participation decisions, loss control decisions and risk financing decisions.

To understand this practically we can consider a new capital investment in a machine for a process. The main variables (or uncertainties) will be:—
— the life of the machine (both physically and in terms of possible obsolescence
— the amount of maintenance and repair needed (amount of work and cost)
— materials and other consumables
— labour costs and other services
— the demand and available price for the product

Looking at this problem:

WE KNOW   — the cost of the machine
               — the cost of materials **now**
               — the cost of labour **now**
               — the present demand and price available

WE DON'T KNOW— how much maintenance and repair will be needed and its cost
               — how long the machine will remain effective
               — how the cost and availability of labour and material will change

In measuring risk we take the available certain information and using available data we make estimates for the future variables. It will be better to use a range of possible results rather than a single figure and helpful to record and explain the reason for our conclusions.

If we consider this problem in regard to calculating insured value we could restate our need. We need to know, calculate or estimate:—
— the cost of replacing the machine if lost (taking into account delivery time, future price and currency change)

— whether the machine would be needed if lost
— whether a similar machine would be available if lost

All organisations will need to insure some of their risks, because the possible financial consequences of non-insurance may be too great. This will require as a minimum calculation of values for insurance taking into account the post-loss financing need. For smaller risks it may also be desired to consider the probability of loss so that a choice can be made between insurance and non-insurance. We are left with the practical need to estimate the possible severity of loss, the likely severity of loss and the associated probabilities. This requires consideration of values exposed, the risks they are exposed to and the circumstances. Chapter II has shown methods of establishing the risks and will help in evaluating the circumstances.

In most organisations schedules of property will be available but prepared for different purposes. The asset records used to determine book value will tend to underestimate the likely loss. The method of depreciation used to calculate book value by taking purchase price and "writing off" part of the price each year assumes that the "value" of the asset decreases each year in money terms. In today's inflationary conditions the "value" of the asset in real terms may rise each year rather than decrease. If it can still do the job it was purchased for and looks capable of continuing in that role for a number of years the measure of "replacement cost" is the price of procuring a similarly capable asset. This could be second-hand if available but may well be a new item of equipment at much greater price.

There are many other considerations:—

1. is it actually possible to purchase another item?
2. would it be cheaper to buy second-hand?
3. what other expenses are associated with replacement?
4. are there any tax considerations such as balancing charge (paying when price of disposal exceeds depreciated value for tax purposes) or balancing allowance for the reverse?
5. is there a better alternative method of operation or purchase?

In using account records a number of corrections or adjustments are needed. The only truly accurate record of value in books of accounts is the cash book showing the amount actually spent and received. The sales ledger may show what is due from a credit customer but there is no guarantee we shall receive or when when we receive it.

It will be obvious that timing of payments or receipts alters their value in two ways:—

1.   If we have the money now we can invest it—so that £1 today may be worth £1.12 in a years time. If a £1 next year is compared with a £1 now there is a 12p difference in next years value in favour of the £1 now.

2.   Inflation will affect both replacement price and the future value of an asset. If the asset can still provide the same facility it may grow in value in £1 terms. 10% inflation may mean an increase in value of .10p.

Some account will need to be taken of both these aspects —the time value of money and inflation—both require assumption of rate of interest earned or rate of inflation.

Discount tables are available to equate money at different periods of time. These are used for many purposes including calculating the present value of a future stream of earnings. Here is an example.

INVEST £10,000	Capital at beginning of year		Interest		Capital at end of year	Equivalent discount factor
in 1 year	10,000	+	1,000	=	11,000	.9091
2 year	11,000	+	1,100	=	12,100	.8264
3 year	12,100	+	1,210	=	13,310	.7513
4 year	13,310	+	1,331	=	14,641	.6830
5 year	14,641	+	1,464	=	16,105	.6209

Therefore (1) to get 10,000 in 5 years we need £6,209
                  (2) £10,000 is worth £6,209

if we have 5 year stream of earnings we have

£10,000 in 1 year	9,091
2 year	8,264
3 year	7,513
4 year	6,830
5 year	6,209
	£37,907

value to us of £10,000 per year for 5 years starting in a years time = £37,907.

However we may not receive £10,000 each year due to changes in business and/or inflation. How we deal with the time value of money is very important in insurance and risk decisions e.g. pre-payment of premiums or delay in payment of claims.

Two other major accounting assumptions that need to be remembered in risk measurement are the treatment of depreciation and the allocation of overheads.

Depreciation is the allowance or charge to current accounts for the use of a machine. It may be charged on an even or straight line basis i.e. 10% per annum—so that all of the cost of the machine has been "written off" at the end of 10 years. Alternatively a balance reducing basis also with 10% will cause a much longer "write-off" always with a residual value.

Depreciation can increase or decrease a years operating profit. It can overstate or understate the actual present (market) value of an asset.

Allocation of overheads is another arbitrary decision. We can try and accurately reflect the spread of general costs over different operating departments but any method is an approximation which may understate or overstate the costs and resulting profit or loss.

Taxation has important effects in risk measurement:—

1. It reduces the effective cost of much expenditure (in terms of net-after-tax cost)
2. It creates another uncertainty for the future—in rate and application of tax
3. There are important differences in the treatment of capital and income
4. Insurance premiums generally provide a tax deductible method of funding for loss.

Having established a value in terms of post-loss financing need we turn to the more difficult problem of risk probabilities. The method used is to examine each risk, its likely and possible effect and the worth of any loss control activity or equipment. Before considering briefly a number of property risk considerations, we need to consider calculation of **estimated maximum loss.**

3.9 EML (estimated maximum loss)

The main practical use of EML (estimated maximum loss) calculations is to assist insurers in establishing the amount of risk that they can retain. The insurer limits his loss from a particular risk by means of reinsurance. Various reinsurance techniques are used such as quota share, surplus, excess loss and stop loss which are described later in section 5.18. Using excess loss reinsurance the insurer undertakes to pay the amount by which a loss exceeds a specified amount, again up to a specified limit.

The acceptance of excess loss reinsurance is thus primarily related to the maximum loss rather than the sum insured (or insured value). Although direct insurance premiums are calculated in relation to sum insured, reinsurance premiums are calculated by reference to the amount of cover in turn related to what is thought to be the maximum loss and the net premium income.

Fire insurance surveys usually include an estimate of the maximum loss expressed either in percentage of property that could be lost or as a financial figure. The survey thus deals with three different but related aspects:—

1. whether the risk is suitable for underwriting acceptance and the terms on which it should be underwritten.

2. risk improvement recommendations, which may well be conditions for underwriting acceptance

3. an estimate of the maximum loss

Only the second part of the survey is normally communicated to the policyholder. Information about maximum loss would be particularly valuable to the risk management adviser.

There is little published information on the calculation of estimated maximum loss and most of the known guidelines deal with physical factors such as type of construction, fire separation and protective systems, rather than an examination of the dynamic circumstances of actual losses. From time to time examples are published in the insurance press of losses where the amount of actual loss was dramatically different from the previously calculated EML.

Some years ago the Reinsurance Offices Association representing most reinsurers in London and the major overseas reinsurers provided a definition of Estimated Maximum Loss (EML) for Fire and Explosion Material Damage as follows:—

"An estimate of the monetary loss which could be sustained by insurers on a single risk as a result of a single fire or explosion considered by the underwriter to be within the realms of probability. The estimate ignores such remote coincidences and catastrophes as may be possibilities but which still remain unlikely".

That definition still leaves a great deal of scope for high severity low probability risks to be ignored—a most dangerous state of affairs. The ROA went on to suggest that where appropriate the total EML could be derived from separate assessment of:—

1. Buildings
2. Machinery and Other Contents
3. Stock especially where contents have a low salvage value or are highly susceptible to damage
4. Risques locatifs and Recours de Voisin (exposure of neighbouring risks—not appropriate in most countries at present)

The Association mentions the following factors to be taken into consideration when assessing the EML on a "single risk":—

1. Size, height and shape of area potentially exposed to a single fire or explosion
2. Construction of roofs, walls and floors
3. Presence of combustible linings to walls, roofs, ceilings and partitions
4. Nature, distribution and combustibility of contents (fire load)
5. Use of hazardous processes and substances and their degree of separation
6. Susceptibility of contents to damage by smoke, heat and water
7. Risk of explosion from any source
8. Hazards arising from gases or corrosive materials
9. Concentration of values within a small area
10. Standards of management and housekeeping

The Association emphasises that the following factors should **not** be taken into account in assessing an EML:

1. Any horizontal separation
2. Fire resisting doors
3. The absence of any normal source of ignition
4. The existence or installation of fire detection, prevention or extinguishment arrangements, including sprinklers and the adequacy or otherwise of fire brigade facilities.

```
RAW
MATERIAL
STORE
0.8
4.1

PRIMARY
PROCESSING

    4.2

    2.0

    3.1
```

```
FINAL
PROCESSING

    2.5

    2.0

    1.3
```

```
MAIN              SPECIAL
PROCESSING        FINISHING

    3.7

    1.2

    .4            PACKAGING
```

```
CAR PARK

    .75
```

```
FINISHED GOODS
WAREHOUSE

              2.6

              1.3

              12.1
```

MAIN ROAD

First Figure   BUILDINGS

Second Figure   PLANT AND MACHINERY

Third Figure   STOCK

CHART 20

Further guidance is given on a "single risk"—

1. On separation between buildings:—

    (a) 15 metres separation with no ⎫ in both cases
        opposing opening, brick, stone ⎪ no intervening
        or concrete walls, slate tile ⎬ combustible
        concrete metal or asbestos ⎪ element
        ceilings ⎭

    or 25 metres separation

    (b) adjacent party walls to be:—
        brick stone or concrete at least 21 cm thick
        no openings
        extending 37 cm above the roof unless the roof
        is concrete on one side

2. For plant in the open or tank storage

    (a) 25 cm between units or tanks

    (b) bunding for 110% of tank capacity

3. Stocks

    (a) total sum insured

    or (b) capacity of biggest single risk

4. Account to be taken of:—

    (a) sloping ground—burning liquid

    (b) explosion

    (c) strong winds

    (d) extreme cold

Despite the ambiguity of the main definition, this material is most helpful in assessing EML.

Charts 20 and 21 show a simple layout plan and values for a simple plant.

Chart 22 shows a chart for recording risk measurement data which closely follows the approach developed in Chapter II.

SUMMARY OF VALUES EXPOSED

	Buildings	Plant & Machinery	Stock	Total
Raw Material Store	0.8	—	4.1	4.9
Primary Processing	4.2	2.0	3.1	9.3
Main Processing Special Finishing Packaging	3.7	1.2	.4	5.3
Final Processing	2.5	2.0	1.3	5.8
Total for Block	11.2	5.2	8.9	25.3

FIRE WALL (*Represents Fire Wall*)

	Buildings	Plant & Machinery	Stock	Total
Finished Goods Warehouse	2.6	1.3	12.1	16.0
		.75		.75
Total for Site	13.8	7.25	21.0	42.05

How could whole block be exposed?

How could more than one block/whole site be exposed?

CHART 21

The main property hazards are as follows:—

FIRE	Accidental/Deliberate On site/Off site
EXPLOSION	Accidental/Deliberate On site/Off site
EARTHQUAKE	(Note goods may be recoverable)
STORM	Apart from flood—main risk to roof
FLOOD	Run-off River
VEHICLE IMPACT ⎫ AIRCRAFT IMPACT ⎭	Possibility of recovery from third party
THEFT	
FRAUD	
MALICIOUS DAMAGE	(other than fire and explosion)

RISK	CIRCUMSTANCES	VALUES EXPOSED	LIMITING FACTORS	AGGRAVATING FACTORS
FIRE	ACCIDENTAL	All of main building 25.3 million	INCEPTION	
	Electrical		Electrical installation modern & checked	
	Process		Process flames enclosed	Difficult to enforce rule 100%
	Smoking		No smoking	
			SPREAD	All fire walls have self-closing doors which might jam or be wedged open
			Fire walls between blocks (primary processing is biggest value 9.3 million)	
			Sprinkler system	
			Works fire brigade	Fire brigade strike
			Local fire brigade at 2 minutes call time	
			DELIBERATE	Annual Shut-down for 3 weeks
			24 hour working	
	DELIBERATE	As above	As above	Sprinkler system:
			Security guard	1. Could be disabled.
				2. Designed to deal with single ignition source. False alarm could increase attendance time to 7 minutes.

CHART 22—RISK MEASUREMENT DATA

For each we can assess the possible and likely extent of vulnerability. It seems to us that the only practical course is to take physical limits only. If it is impossible for fire to travel from one block to another then we can limit the EML to one block only for accidental fire. This would only be true for deliberate fire if we were dealing with an unambitious or incompetent arsonist. In considering EML (and risk identification) we need a pessimistic imagination. For example we have talked about limiting fire to one block because of adequate fire separation but we need to consider the materials on site. A very large loss at a small chemical refinery resulted from burning flowing wax moving the fire from its point of origin down a slight slope to the other parts of the plant.

3.10 Fire Risk Measurement

There is a great deal more work we can do if it makes economic sense. We can study the inception hazard for electrical and process ignition in terms of failure rate. We can measure the fire load in terms of calorific value of materials. It is also possible to calculate the smoke and fumes released on the same basis—in many fires smoke and fumes are a major hazard to employees and fire-fighters as well as being the cause of damage to goods otherwise unaffected by the fire.

The energy equivalent of the fire (calorific value) can be used to calculate extinguishing needs.

Chart 23 suggests some of the main aspects of measuring fire risks.

3.11 Explosion Risk Measurement

We can similarly calculate explosion results theoretically which can help in devising effective loss control as well as estimating the maximum loss. In assessing explosion effects we need to distinguish between different types of explosion.

Chart 24 shows the different types of explosion.

The effect of an explosion can be estimated by calculating the energy available either chemically or physically and translating this into an over-pressure. By plotting the over-pressure on plans of the area around the likely explosion centre we can calculate the resultant effects in terms of danger to buildings and their occupants.

FIRE

INCEPTION HAZARD SOURCES OF IGNITION	Electrical Process—Failure rate Smoking Maintenance regular—irregular Deliberate single—multiple Other external
FIRE LOAD BUILDING	Walls Frame Roof Lining Doors
EQUIPMENT MATERIAL }	Regular Unusual
FUEL	Gas/Oil
DISCOVERY	Automatic—Manual Manning—Operation times
FIRE FIGHTING	Available water flow—Duration
POSSIBLE BUILD UP PATTERN	Sprinkler—Non Sprinkler (Non operating) Local fire fighting attendance time and capability Brigade fire fighting attendance time and capability Physical (containment) limits Separation and/or Fire Load

CHART 23 FIRE RISK MEASUREMENT FACTORS

An important secondary effect of confined explosions (either completely or partially) is the "missile" effect from high velocity pieces of debris. These can cause injury or damage at considerable distances from the point of origin of the explosion. At the moment there seems no practical method of estimating their effect. Study of many large explosions shows large numbers of near misses where such missiles "narrowly missed" people and key items of equipment. It has been suggested on the basis of practical experience that the secondary explosion effect from missiles is small but we would recommend consideration and measurement of the effect of loss of a second unit from secondary explosion (and if it seems warranted the third unit also).

TYPES OF EXPLOSION

Chemical — Resulting from chemical change.

  (1) DEFLAGRATION — Exothermic reaction propagating (in similar manner to fire) by conduction, convection or radiation to unreacted material. Combustion zone moves through unreacted material at rate less than speed of sound.

  (2) DETONATION — Exothermic reaction propagating by shock wave in/from source material. Heat effect is by shock compression. Combustion zone moves through unreacted material at rate greater than speed of sound.

Chemical Explosions

  (A) DEFLAGRATION OR DETONATION OF GAS — Gas and vapour-air mixtures have limits of flammability and detonability. Below limit mixture is too weak and above limit mixture is too rich.
NOTE these are not alternatives— both may occur in same material at different temperatures and pressures.

  (B) DEFLAGRATION OF DUST — Not all dusts are explosive. Smaller particles increase surface area and ease of ignition. Note double effect — small explosion disturbs dust creates conditions for large explosion.

  (C) DEFLAGRATION OF MIST — Droplets of flammable liquids.

  (D) DECOMPOSITION — Includes regular explosives and similar substances.

Physical or Mechanical — Explosive release of pressure e.g. bursting of boiler due to excessive pressure, bursting of gas cylinder due to corrosion of vessel.

Atomic — Nuclear reactions.

CHART 24—TYPES OF EXPLOSION

3.12 Earthquake Risk Measurement

Most of the risk in fire and explosion arises from man-made activity — for earthquake man's only contribution is the extent of earthquake loss control used in siting and construction of buildings for example.

For the risk management specialist the first factor is the existence of an exposure and its significance. Theoretically there is an earthquake risk everywhere but our records (over a relatively limited timespan) have permitted the production of fairly accurate maps showing sites exposed to earthquakes with their past severity and frequency.

The modified Intensity Scale as rewritten by Richter gives a useful reference scale.

After reviewing the exposure to earthquake one needs to consider the susceptibility of the building or other structure to loss. Earthquake building codes exist in many cities subject to frequent shock (such as Wellington, New Zealand) or catastrophic shock (such as San Francisco). Two main effects need to be considered, the earth-shifting in the area of the fault and the vibration felt over a wide area. Most codes involve resistance to "shaking".

A similar approach can be adopted to volcanoes — government assistance is often available to risk management as with the Government Volcanologist in New Zealand. Another associated exposure is the large tidal wave associated with earthquakes such as the Tsunami in Hawaii — a similar approach is recommended.

3.13 Storm Risks

Storm risk includes the effect of high winds and large rainfalls. Meteorological records provide data on previously experienced winds but the most serious problem is assessing the ability of modern structures to withstand winds. Unfortunately the only useful and reliable guide is long term experience. Wind tunnel testing is interesting but there seems to be a divergence between theory and practice. The risk management adviser should be on the lookout for all forms of light-weight structure, especially roofs. Most storm damage relates to roofs but other collapsing structures may affect vital or expensive equipment. Often the consequential loss affects of storms are much greater.

In terms of practical risk management building codes and the establishment of proper procedures for action before and during storms should limit the loss in hurricane and typhoon areas. Some of the biggest losses have occurred in areas where it was felt that the risk "did not exist" or "was not serious".

3.14   Flood Risk

A key element in defensive risk management is lateral thinking to produce more fundamental definitions that force wider consideration. Flood is simply water (or occasionally another liquid) in the wrong place in significant quantities. Too often it is thought of as rivers overflowing. It is true that swollen rivers are a major cause of flood but there are many others related to water run-off.

Measuring the flood risk requires understanding the water flow and routes during normal and abnormal weather conditions. Previous rainfall records are only directly relevant where there has been no change in the river basin or surrounding countryside.

Changes in land-use, particularly the covering of soil by concrete and buildings and associated drainage schemes often add to the flood hazard. This recurs because the run-off is re-routed; more reaches the river and at much faster rates (sometimes 1,000 times). At government level a technique has been developed for photographing river basins to calculate the increased risk. Most water-control schemes involve a measure of calculated risk — and regrettably most of them do not anticipate future change.

At a lower level industrial estates provide a particular flood hazard. Occupation by different industries with different water usage may create overload conditions — most local authorities do not calculate the effect of changes of use on run-off levels.

3.15   Theft Risk

In a modern industrial society theft represents a significant and unnecessary cost burden which can be reduced and controlled by risk management. In measuring theft risk we have several sources of data:—

1.   theft loss experience—although one needs to remember that this only records "discovered" theft

2.   opportunities for theft—what is worth stealing and can be stolen

3.   what controls exist and how effective are they.

One interesting aspect of risk studies is that frequently they reveal areas of theft loss about which management was ignorant. The reasons for this include the characteristics of modern budget systems—once a level of loss has been built in to the budget it will automatically inflate with it. Most internal thefts are only discovered when they exceed certain limits.

Appraisal of stock and other control systems will often show existing or potential theft risk.

3.16 Fraud

One of the biggest areas of risk for any company is fraud and particularly that associated with electronic data processing. Measurement of risk consists of:—

1. establishing amounts at risks
2. determining circumstances in which fraud can take place
3. assessing effectiveness of controls

When measuring fraud risk one should give precedence to opportunity; it should not be assumed from personal knowledge of senior office holders that there is no risk.

The risk management process can add to this danger if care is not taken to keep records to a minimum and tightly control circulation of notes that describe systems and risks. There is a brief reference to computer risk management in Chapter VII.

3.17 Earnings Risk Measurement

Following our pattern of linking the treatment of risk to insurable risk we can identify consequential loss exposures under three main heads:—

1. pre-tax earnings that are lost as a result of the risk event
2. loss of recovery of overheads due to the risk event
3. special expenditure after-loss

A financial example may show the effects. Our factory has an annual turnover of £102 million and profits of £13 million. Raw material and other variable costs account for £42 million of the £89 million overall cost. Our fixed costs which include our labour force are £47 million.

A fire at our major supplier causes a reduction in turnover of 60% for 6 months (102m. × 60% × 50% = £30.6 loss of turnover). There is a saving of variable cost of £42m.

× 60% × 50% = £12.6m. This would result in a shortfall of both income and costs but the effect on costs would be much smaller.

Our turnover for the period will be £20.4 million.

Our costs for the period will be £31.9 million.

This will produce a loss of £11.5 million but our loss compared with expected result will be:—

LOSS OF PRE-TAX EARNINGS OF	£6.5 MILLION
UNRECOVERED OVERHEAD	£11.5 MILLION
	£18 MILLION

If we found that by spending £3 million we could secure a further 25% of turnover it would have the effect of:

TURNOVER (£102m. × 65% × 50%)	= £33.15m.
VARIABLE COST (£42m. × 65% × 50%)	= £13.65m.
FIXED COST	£23.5 m.

When added to the special expenditure of £5 million this will produce costs for the period of £42.15 and our loss is reduced to £9 million. In terms of the three categories we now have.

LOSS OF PRE-TAX EARNINGS	£6.5m.
UNRECOVERED OVERHEADS	£4m.
	(Turnover less fixed and variable cost)
SPECIAL EXPENSE	£5m.

Measuring the earnings risk involves:—

1. Charting the external dependencies — supplier and customer
2. Listing the key internal dependencies — each stage of the process
3. Calculating the ultimate earnings dependency on each risk event in 1 and 2.
4. Considering alternative action which could reduce loss.

Chart 25 gives a simple earnings check-list and a simplified chart for consequential loss contingency planning appears in Chapter IV.

Three main exposures:
1. pre-tax earnings
2. loss of recovery of overhead
3. special expenditure after-loss

List main process stages

Note earnings dependency at each stage

Include main suppliers of goods and services and main customers

What events can cause interruption?

In what circumstances?

Which are the key dependencies? (highest exposure)

How would we handle interruption?
— replace?
— substitute?

What is
— the likely loss?
— the maximum loss?

How much would replacement/substitution cost?

CHART 25—EARNINGS RISK MEASUREMENT

3.18 Liability Risk Measurement

The measurement of liability risk is the most difficult problem of risk measurement. We can see our property exposures and value them. Even to find all the risk possibilities does not seem impossible. Our liability exposure is everywhere — every action of every employee has the possibility of a liability claim.

More seriously the size of the claim is not related to our culpability — it depends on the loss to the other party. The same mistake (on say an airfield) may cause a small fire or the loss of several aircraft and terminal buildings perhaps running to several hundred million pounds.

We show in Chart 26 a simple liability check list. It should be noted that we may have (in some circumstances) limitation of liability. To take a pessimistic view our biggest loss is total loss of all our assets.

From a short examination it will be seen that the main value of liability risk measurement is to improve awareness of the risk inside the company. It will help us to decide the level of insurance cover needed — we can then assess to what extent we can afford it.

We can measure property/earnings exposure with some accuracy — liability is much harder.

Is liability limited?

— in what circumstances?

Consider the circumstances

— activity/operation
— product/service
— use/misuse
— location (always look at the worst circumstances)

When will legal award be made?

— whose jurisdiction?
— how will law have changed?
— how will legal climate have changed?

How much do we have (assets) in all?

— that is our potential for loss (ultimately).

CHART 26—SIMPLE CHART FOR REVIEWING EXTENT OF LIABILITY RISK

Chapter IV contains more information on the character and control of liability risk.

Chapter IV

Risk Control

4.1 Managing Risk

The concept of risk management implies a positive approach to risk. Firstly recognising risk as implicit in all our activities so that we cannot completely avoid it. Secondly adopting a conscious risk decision-making process where we attempt to recognise and measure the risks threatening our activities as a preliminary to accepting, transferring eliminating or reducing the risks and their impact.

Acceptance of risk may be the best course where the consequences are trivial and the cost of elimination or control relatively expensive.

Transfer of risk is a somewhat misleading term and involves confusion between risk and its financial consequences. There may be circumstances where we can transfer the actual risk by getting someone else to undertake the dangerous activity; but usually risk transfer is applied to the transfer of the financial consequences. This transfer could take place by another party being legally bound to accept the financial consequences which might be for our injury, loss or damage, our loss of earnings or against the liability claims of others.

Insurance is often regarded as a transfer of risk but technically it is normally only a partial transfer of risk as some of the financial consequences of a loss may not be recoverable from insurers.

This chapter deals primarily with the elimination or reduction of risk by risk control methods although risk transfer is partially dealt with at the end of the chapter.

4.2 The Approach to Risk Control

For many insurable risks such as fire, explosion and theft

a great deal of valuable technical literature is available describing the "hardware" of loss control. By "hardware" we mean the physical equipment that can be made available to eliminate or reduce loss. We see no advantage in repeating such material but instead concentrate on the "risk management" approach.

In presenting risk management as a conscious risk control activity we would focus on the key role of people in managing risk. Relatively few risks arise from causes that do not directly involve man (such as earthquake and lightning) but even for these risks their effect is of course directly related to man's activities. We can arrange our affairs so that we can take account of possible serious risk threats or ignore them.

All of the "hardware" used for loss control is dependent on man's understanding and willingness to control risk. A fire hose or extinguisher needs someone to use it. The human decision as to what type of hose or extinguisher and location will seriously affect the capability to control or put out the fire. Even an automatic sprinkler depends on proper analysis of the fire load, advice of significant change, maintenance and freedom from interference to be effective when needed.

These examples show one side of human involvement in risk control, the need to make the right decision by good anticipation and technical skill. In many risk situations we are concerned either with indifferent human activity (indifferent in the sense of not being committed to use every resource to protect assets) or with malicious human activity.

With the increasing size and fragmentation of responsibility in modern industry it is easy for a situation to arise where the person nearest to a loss situation feels it is not his responsibility to do anything about it — indeed he may not know what to do. Apart from ignorance, in some organisations alienation has led to hostility to the enterprise and its assets manifested in lack of care or concern.

Protection of people and assets against criminal activity depends on understanding the "criminal" and his likely activities and reactions. Because these activities involve human beings who are flexible and imaginative, we face the possibility that our control measures may rebound upon us. Information we collect may become available for criminal use, the existence of special locks etc. may alert the criminal to an opportunity, or the hardware (locks, safes etc.) and software (security systems employed) may be treated as a challenge. Any control measure in such a human situation is at best temporary in its effectiveness.

4.3 Risk Control Objectives

Before undertaking risk control activity we need to define our objectives. We can divide the main situations into three:—

1. injury to people

2. regular material loss

3. irregular, infrequent and catastrophic material loss.

For human beings our sense of humanity will demand that our only objective should be no injury or death although our sense of reality will tell us that in many circumstances that is impossible. It is difficult to give any guidelines for risk control objectives other than nil where human beings are concerned but we can add some comment.

An American psychologist has suggested that in general we are willing to accept about 1,000 times more risk voluntarily than the risk we are prepared to have thrust upon us. This fact upsets a number of groups including the chemical industry who often compare the relative safety of the chemical industry with many other dangerous activities such as road travel and several sports.

For those concerned with setting standards in human safety we can perceive that public opinion often sets standards. The large and very productive expenditure on air safety which has improved the risk in frequency terms by about 16 times in the last 30 years results from an almost universal fear of flying. However it should not be thought that airlines or aircraft manufacturers will spend without limit. A number of measures that would improve air safety further await either general agreement or the equipment or sufficient pressure from Government or press or public opinion.

Increasing interest in safety has increased the volume and improved the quality of accident statistics and for fatal injuries we have the fatal accident frequency rate (FAFR) as a guideline. Our aim might well be expressed as continuing to improve this rate overall, and for specific industries aiming to produce results better than the overall FAFR with urgent attention where we have higher casualty rates.

Regular material loss does not present a problem for objectives. We can measure what we are losing and spend more money in preventing some of this loss where it is economically justified (where amount spent on more loss control is significantly less than the cost of losses saved). It is important to take a broad view. For example quite small material losses may have a much greater effect on our market reputation and sales.

The irregular, infrequent, catastrophic loss presents a more difficult task. Measured in terms of estimated expectancy it may seem of little likelihood and therefore consequence, but if it occurs it will be disastrous. Some loss control expenditure will be required as a result of government regulations and insurance requirements. Further loss control may be felt expedient to confirm with generally accepted industry standards.

A catastrophic fire or explosion is likely to involve human life either directly or indirectly (e.g. to toxic fumes) and result in official enquiry. If the company sets out to put themselves in a position where they can effectively defend their loss control they have probably taken all the logical loss control steps.

All risk control decisions tend to be trade-off decisions. We spend a definite amount now for expected benefits later. These benefits may be in terms of either a reduced probability of loss or a reduced size of loss. It has already been noted that it is difficult, if not impossible, to quantify the benefits from a reduction in the probability of an already very low probability catastrophic loss. Consequently such risk control decisions tend utility decisions answering the questions "What is it worth to me/us to reduce the expected possibility of size of loss?".

4.4 Strategy of Loss Control

Accidents have been succinctly described as energy in the wrong place. William Haddon, an American epidemiologist has drawn up an analysis of strategies for reducing losses based on containing the release of energy or its effects.

Chart 27 is based on Haddon's analysis. It provides the basis for a relatively comprehensive approach permitting the risk management adviser to analyse the loss event and compare alternative methods of achieving the same objective.

Haddon's approach is based on technical analysis altering the structure of the activity to reduce the loss potential. Unlike most safety work it is not based on appeals to be good but on making it easy to do the right thing and difficult to do the wrong thing.

A different approach was used by a well-known safety expert H. W. Heinrich in his book "Industrial Accident Prevention" when he demonstrated that an accident results from a chain of events each leading to the rest. He compared the chain with a group of dominoes, each one knocking the next over and suggested that by taking away one of the dominoes the accident would be prevented. Chart 28 shows Heinrich's summary.

Heinrich attached greatest importance to the third stage "the unsafe act" and therefore his followers focus on human error. This was not so much on the basis that human error was the main cause of accidents but that he felt it was easier to remove this reason for accidents.

A study of accident reports such as official investigations into major failures, big explosions, ship and aircraft accidents will invariably show that each event had a number of contributing factors. Removal of a single factor would either have prevented the loss or significantly reduced its scale.

4.5 Human Error

As most accidents and losses inevitably involve the results of man's actions it is a reasonable assumption that human error is a factor in each accident and loss. A great deal of time and energy is spent telling people to be good and human error tends to be thought of in terms of blame implying that if we were good accidents would not happen.

Attention is now being given to analysis of "human error" to try and establish why the "human" made the "error". Perhaps not surprisingly it has been found that some errors are very easy to make and difficult not to make.

Pilot error was regarded as the major cause of air accidents, conveniently in many cases as the pilot was dead and could not argue. Some years ago Strategic Air

STRATEGY	EXAMPLE
Prevent the marshalling of energy whose release could lead to loss	Manufacture of gunpowder Accumulation of snow for avalanche Elevation of skiers Location of baby above floor in chair
Reduce amount of energy marshalled	Limit reacting chemicals in schools Size of fireworks Height of divers above swimming pools Speed of vehicles
Prevent release of energy	Prevent discharge of nuclear bombs Discharge of electricity Fall of lifts Jumping of would-be suicides
Modify rate or spatial distribution of release of energy	Reduce slope of beginners ski trails Slower burning explosives Select re-entry speed and trajectory for space vehicles
Separate in space or time energy released from susceptible structure	Separation of pedestrians from vehicles by barriers Lightning conductors Traffic control
Separation by interposition of material barrier energy from susceptible structure	Safety shoes and other equipment Armour plate
Modify contact surface to reduce injury or damage	Eliminate, round, soften corners, edges and sharp points
Strengthen structure that is subject to damage	Building codes for earthquakes Training for athletes Vaccines
Rapidly detect, evaluate damage and counter continuation and extension	Alarm systems
Action after damaging energy exchange to reduce loss	Disaster planning Any action to restore previous or new equilibrium

CHART 27—STRATEGIES FOR REDUCING LOSS

as devised by William Haddon Jr. M.D. 1970

1. Ancestry and social environment

Recklessness, stubbornness, avariciousness, and other undesirable traits of character may be passed along through inheritance.

Environment may develop undesirable traits of character or may interfere with education. Both inheritance and environment cause faults of person.

2. Fault of person

Inherited or acquired faults of person; such as recklessness, violent temper, nervousness, excitability, inconsiderateness, ignorance of safe practice etc., constitute proximate reasons for commiting unsafe acts or for the existence of mechanical or physical hazards.

3. Unsafe act and/or mechanical or physical hazard

Unsafe performance of persons, such as standing under suspended loads, starting machinery without warning, horseplay, and removal of safeguards; and mechanical or physical hazards, such as unguarded gears, unguarded point of operation, absence of rail guards, and insufficient light, result directly in accidents.

4. Accident

Events such as falls of persons, striking of persons by flying objects etc., are typical accidents that cause injury.

5. Injury

Fractures, lacerations etc., are injuries that result directly from accidents.

CHART 28—HEINRICH ANALYSIS OF ACCIDENT FACTORS

Command of the USAF abolished pilot error as an acceptable reason for an accident and suggested that alternatives should be found. The alternatives to "human error" would include:—

1.   Poor design
2.   Poor system
3.   Poor training
4.   Poor staff selection

Poor design is unfortunately all around us. Two identical switches need not cause a problem if they switch on two different lights in a room but next to each other in an aircraft cockpit to be used in totally different circumstances they could be lethal. There were many red faces in the oil industry when it was discovered that a key piece of equipment involved in the "Bravo" blowout at Ekofisk was fitted upside down—not just because it was fitted the wrong way up but because it was designed in such a way that it could be fitted two ways. We still read of unfortunate victims of hospital mistakes where the wrong gas is connected.

Risk management involves asking the question "Why" many times and pursuing the real cause of accidents so that we can build "foolproof" equipment for we are all fools at times. There are still many industrial situations that place impossible demands on operators in terms of expecting constant alertness in a very boring job, of requiring skills greater than those available, or creating a conflict between production (and sometimes bonuses) and safety.

4.6   Risk Management and People

Risk management is essentially concerned with events that disrupt (or could disrupt) the pattern of future earnings or performance of individuals or organisations and thereby expose people or assets to loss. We can classify events giving rise to this disruption under two main headings e.g.:—

(a) **events external to man.** These events might be controllable, partially controllable or beyond man's control. A typical example would be lightning which we can partially control the effects of by earthing procedures and equipment. Another example is earthquake. Whilst we are experimenting with releasing the tension between geological plates that cause earthquakes when violently released most practical work is concerned with controlling effects through use of building codes etc.

A further example is flood where effects can be controlled by location of buildings, drainage or water diversion systems.

(b) **resulting from man's action.** We can sub-divide this into three other categories:—

   (i)   **deliberate**—actions intended to harm. The results of such deliberate harmful action might well be different from those expected by perpetrators or victims. Examples are arson, hijacking, kidnap, terrorism and vandalism.

   (ii)   **inadvertent**—losses resulting from lack of care or any situation where the result is (negatively) different from that intended. Examples include poor design, poor manufacture, poor planning, poor control or lack of response to external hazards.

   (iii)   completely accidental (after intervention that is neither deliberate or inadvertent) such as losses resulting from lack of technical knowledge. The series of Comet I airliner crashes resulting from pressurisation failure in turn due to lack of necessary technical knowledge beforehand on the part of the aviation industry.

(Losses resulting from these three categories are largely controllable in full or part BUT the cost of control may be excessive).

Most crime falls in category (b) (i) above although the area covered by (b) (i) does not coincide with the area described as crime due to the problem of labelling crime. This arises because crimes are given a legal definition to permit the operation of legal processes. This definition may not cover or coincide with all deliberate harmful acts. Additionally it may not be possible to prove that a known event is a "crime" due to lack of evidence.

As inadvertent (i.e. non-deliberate) action may be technically a crime such as momentary lack of attention leading to a charge of "driving without due care or attention".

All crime by its very nature must involve people. Both criminal and non-criminal human action add considerably to the complexity and difficulty of practical risk management. We can take technical steps to limit risk and its effects but our efforts may be frustrated, hindered or augmented by deliberate and inadvertent action.

In considering the actions (behaviour) of people in a risk sense there are various inherent factors other than the physical circumstances of the event (or crime) such as:—

(a) does the individual understand risk? e.g. is he/she acquainted with and able to estimate/evaluate risk?

(b) is it an active or passive acceptance of risk or conscious or unconscious?

(c) what is the risk attitude of the individual? Do they like/enjoy or hate risk?

(d) how is the particular risk regarded by the population as a whole or specific groups of the population?

(e) does the population as a whole/specific groups want to manage/control the risk?

(f) how does the individual make the "trade-off" decision? (here we mean the balancing of positive and negative factors in taking or ignoring the risk. We might regard the enjoyment of a particular sport as more valuable than the negative aspect of the possibility of serious injury. Or in terms of crime the balance between possible penalty and likely benefit for the criminal and possible inconvenience etc. and likely benefit for the potential intervention to prevent a crime).

All human actions involving risk including crime take place in a fast changing world. Many of the factors of change have a big impact on crime trends and patterns such as:—

(a) improved instant communication ranging from data to role of the media as a trigger for crime.

(b) larger economic units creating greater vulnerability to risk threats. This includes all eggs in one basket (e.g. one warehouse replacing several; most computer systems) and ease of disruption for many technically complex systems. These larger economic units also break down the feeling of caring and responsibility and lead to feelings of alienation on the part of the workforce, customers and the general public.

(c) for sectors of the world's population, the main material needs have been satisfied. This creates a number of secondary effects including, for a minority, an overall questioning of the role of society. Another effect is that examined by Fred Hirsch in "Social Limits to Growth" as increasing affluence leads to seeking of impossible goals such as

  (i)   more space—suburbia cripples itself
  (ii) individual motor transport—reduced mobility due to traffic jams and parking problems
  (iii) holidays in Spain lose their value due to over-crowding.

(d) limited resources to meet expanded aims. We are facing shortages of some key raw materials (see reaction to shortages caused by strikes to anticipate possible future reaction). A big increase in relative price of some types of labour has made a number of previously viable activities almost economically impossible e.g. new underground railways.

(e) greater role of government and large scale private business (which reproduces some of the negative bureaucratic features of government) is distorting social and economic trends. The growth of the social services reduces voluntary work and may well lead to greater alienation. There is less opportunity for enterprising satisfying work despite the rise in resources.

(f) changes in the domestic situation, in particular changing family values which are less cohesive for the greater family with fewer local relations and in many cases for the smaller family due to more work demands.

(g) neighbourhood changes with the break-up of local close groups and in the type of household units such as the replacement of small city streets by tower blocks and suburbia both leading to remoteness.

Crime trends therefore need to be related to changes in society including:

(a) economically with evaluation of crime as an occupation (full or part-time) providing an alternative to other methods of employment or acquisition.

(b) socially with less feeling of responsibility. In relation to property it is more likely to:

  (i)   belong to remote (unknown) people or larger organisations
  (ii) to be taken care of by people who feel no personal responsibility for it in absence of owners (private individual, private group or "public").

In considering risk aspects of crime we should note the growing (and almost universal?) recognition by criminologists that the criminal is not a special category of social deviant. Rather it would seem that we are all (in fact or potentially) criminals. To illustrate this we might consider the following behaviour which must be criminal or tending to criminal thoughts or behaviour:—

(a) use of our employer's equipment, material and time (to put this in perspective we might also consider criminal acts of employers in abuse of employee's).

(b) politically "justified" acts of outrage.

(c) resentment at the behaviour of others.

(d) unreasonable persuasion in selling/getting business or jobs.

(e) dishonesty or otherwise in advertising

(f) bribery/corruption/inducements

(We could take this three much wider and examine the universal or new-universal acceptances of a number of sins perhaps in relation to a simple code such as The Ten Commandments).

Ignoring the aspect of technical "inadvertent" crime, criminals as people might have an interest in frustrating the risk management process. This means that instead of seeing risk management as a process of identifying, measuring and controlling the risk we need to take into account the reaction of criminals to each part of the process:—

(a) our identification and measurement can assist the criminal by drawing his attention to opportunities and advising him of our assessment of the crime threat

(b) own control measures may similarly draw attention to criminal opportunities and our control system thus helping the criminal to defeat it.

— recognising the present character of crime
— assessing the "trade-off" for the criminal
— trying to determine the factors encouraging the growth of crime
— reviewing the crime prevention and control "trade-off" to establish:

(a) whether further investment would be justified

(b) whether a change in investment would be profitable.

For all new and changed methods of crime prevention and control we need to estimate how the criminal will or could react.

Accepting crime as a risk management problem the problem can be stated very simply as:—

discouraging the criminal (or rather discouraging criminal tendencies)

making his job more difficult we could see this in terms of:

denying or reduction	INFORMATION
limiting or preventing	ACCESS
limiting or preventing	LACK OF INTERFERENCE before/during/after execution of crime
making his	TASK more difficult requiring more skill time tools data
denying	SUPPORT (increasing hostility)

If the primary motivation is ECONOMIC this discouragement may cause him to:—

(1) give up crime

(2) change his criminal activity (to an area that provides a better reward/effort ratio)

(3) undergo further training

(4) develop new methods to frustrate our efforts

If the primary motivation is NON-ECONOMIC he may:

(1) give up reward/efforts ratio too poor

(2) try harder

(3) alter his activity
(reward in this context is any measure of his satisfaction at the result. If the reward is a feeling of success against adversity new control measures might actually reinforce rather than reduce his effort).

In assessing risk in relation to people and their behaviour sociological and psychological aspects including:—

(a) **transformation in society and its effect** e.g. war and peace. A "patriotic" war results in collective fervour. Some activities which would be considered criminal in peacetime are openly encouraged in wartime and various "criminal" skills are made use of. This tends to lead to a sharp reduction in ordinary "legal" categories of crime. One major exception needs to be made —the breakdown of orderly society during actual **act** of occupation often or usually accompanied by rape or pillage in turn followed by strict enforcement of martial law.

(b) **role of frustration** in loosening bonds. The individual respects a society (wide-natural or local-family or company) that achieves or helps one achieve ones ambitions and aims. Frustration can also result from individuals incompetence in understanding society or a particular situation. We can either view society as wrong or see the individual as failing to relate. This could lead to a "risk management approach" in terms of improving individual's competence to deal with and relate to society/situation he or she is in.

Finally there is an urgent need to fit the recognition, evaluation and management of risk into a "systems" setting so that we can see secondary effects and reactions.

4.7   Loss Experience as an Aid to Loss Control

Our own and other people's accidents and losses provide a fund of useful experience that we can put to good use to avoid accidents. In analysing each accident we shall set out to discover all the significant factors. Taking each factor in turn we should evaluate how easy or difficult it would be to control the factor economically. When a change looks desirable we need to check through all the primary and secondary effects it might have, taking into account human behaviour.

One of the biggest problems in keeping loss control standards at a high level is to maintain alertness. Most of the time we are not having a loss at our particular place of work and a major catastrophe we are unlikely to experience. However, we are frequently in conditions that could lead to a loss and from time to time in conditions that could lead to a catastrophe. Circulation of loss details help keep the possibility in mind and by adding to our knowledge, and to our capability to prevent loss or catastrophe.

Earlier in the book we showed a pyramid of losses with frequent small losses at the base and the infrequent catastrophic loss at the top. We can add to this diagram a further base layer—of incidents that did not lead to loss but might have resulted in loss if other circumstances had been different.

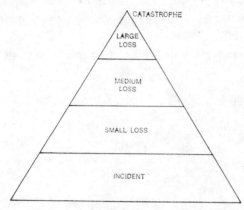

Such incidents are much more frequent than accidents and provide us with a broader statistical loss control base. An incident could be the unexpected failure of a key item of equipment or some human mistake. Considerable use is made in aviation of incident reporting to improve the reliability of equipment, and redesign equipment and systems in the light of experience. Frequently we are dealing with a combination of factors not realised or not taken into account at the design stage.

4.8   How Does Risk Arise?

Chart 29 shows a simple system for factor analysis, which can be used in conjunction with Haddon's approach in Chart 27. We have divided the factors into two—passive and active.

Under the heading passive we have included all the physical facilities, building, plant, equipment and stock when not in use. We need to consider any hazards implicit in these passive resources in terms of heights, dangerous projections, dangerous materials etc.

Most of the risk arises in relation to the **active factors** arising from activities which we engage in. In conducting a risk audit it is helpful to analyse each activity and its hazards —as shown in Chart 29. It should be noted that the chart is dated (circumstances may change) and that it is prepared by the risk management adviser and checked by line management.

Other important aspects to bear in mind are:—

1. Activity off the site that could cause a hazard on site.

2. Unofficial or unauthorised activity.

3. How the position varies according to shift, time of day and season.

4. Unusual circumstances that could increase the risk e.g. visits.

How does risk arise?   —   factor analysis

Property hazard

building

plant

passive   equipment

stock

activity (inside/outside)

(normal/abnormal)

active   timing

circumstances

Can we control the risks?

design   — organisation
           — system
           — building/plant/equipment

protection — equipment
           — systems

people   — training
           — motivation
           — monitoring

CHART 29—RISK FACTOR ANALYSIS

ACTIVITY	EQUIPMENT INVOLVED	OPERATIONS INVOLVED	HAZARDS	COMMENTS

RISK FACTOR ANALYSIS

SITE:

DATE:

ANALYSIS CARRIED THROUGH BY: (risk management advisers)

CHECKED BY: (line management)

CHART 30—RISK FACTOR ANALYSIS

4.9   Systematic Loss Control

Having recorded the loss inducing factors we need to determine our course of action. The measures that we undertake can have any one or more of the following effects:—

1.   Reduce possibility of loss occurring.

2.   Reduce severity of loss when it occurs.

3.   Limit impact of loss event on our operations and resources.

These three effects can be linked to three different time phases, pre-event, during event and post-event, although all our activity is pre-meditated and therefore pre-event.

4.9   Economic Loss Control

In our definition of risk management we used the expression **economic** control. Therefore we need to make sure that our loss control is economic as well as systematic.

This means assessing the cost of losses and the cost of loss control measures. We should be able to evaluate the economic effect by measuring the reduction in losses achieved by each loss control measure.

It is easy to underestimate the cost of losses. The main factors to be included are:—

1.   direct property cost (replacement and repair)

2.   any earnings lost by non-availability of the item of property

3.   loss of management and other time:
     (a) at time of loss
     (b) subsequently in investigation, reporting, replacement

4.   loss of sales through non-availability of equipment

For major losses there are other factors such as delay in replacing due to investigation, the need to meet new regulations and standards.

In making the comparison between loss control expenditure and losses saved (or reduction in cost) there is no problem with regular frequent loss but we also spend to reduce possibility and severity of large losses. To some extent any assessment of probability (before and after) is very subjective but the attempt to quantify should still be made. The cost of the loss control measure will be known. The effect should be estimated in two parts:

1. the probability and likely severity before the particular loss control is instituted

2. the probability and likely severity after the loss control measure is implemented

We should critically review these estimates, not with the intention of discouraging loss control activity but ensuring that the expenditure is cost effective.

Chart 31 shows a simple check list for Economic Loss Control.

ECONOMIC loss control

— **calculate cost of losses** — direct

— indirect

estimate future cost

record assumptions

— **calculate cost of each loss control measure**

— direct

— indirect

— **estimate future benefit**

in cost of losses avoided   } direct
in cost of losses reduced   } indirect

record assumptions

In reduced probability of large loss: how does the saving arise?

— **classify loss control measures**

in order of — economic pay off

— acceptability

— durability: how long will they last?

CHART 31—ECONOMIC LOSS CONTROL

One of the major differences that risk management brings to loss control is a broader view of the loss control activity in particular a recognition of the difference between the instigation of loss control measures and their practical effect. In reviewing loss control activity we can distinguish between **passive** loss control, which does not require positive action to make it work (although it may be affected by human action) and **active** loss control which requires active human participation.

Some examples may help to show the difference. Fire separation measures are largely passive—we do not need to take any further action for it to take effect. However, other activity may intervene—a good separation between two stacks of timber may be negated by filling the intervening space with loaded timber lorries (perhaps a not unlikely action in a busy timber yard overnight).

Hose reels are an important loss control device but they need further action to be effective. People have to be trained to use them, they need to be connected to the water supply, protected for deterioration and damage and people are needed at the time of the fire.

The human intervention in loss control can take many forms:—

1. understanding and commitment to use effectively
2. lack of understanding—good intentions can be spoilt
3. lack of commitment—unconcern about loss or fear of possible danger
4. attempt to frustrate loss control

If we see loss control as a circle it will be appreciated that any break in our circle will cause loss of effective loss control action.

Training in loss control will permit acquisition of the necessary skills, develop competence and overcome hesitancy. It is no good expecting staff to evacuate a multi-storey building through external staircases unless they have already had experience in non-emergency conditions. Incidentally these drills often show that problems would be experienced in emergency conditions such as lack of marking, unsuitable footwear and perhaps insufficient size of exits.

Sometimes training in loss control can have an exactly opposite effect and cause an increase in losses. An explanation of fire or other hazards may induce interest and activity in causing fire or other loss because the person concerned is hostile to the organisation, to create excitement, out of curiosity or to gain personal attention.

In one case teaching school children more about fire had the effect of increasing their capability to burn their schools. In this situation removal of fire load and ignition sources is more effective but might be much more expensive.

Loss control motivation is one of the most neglected areas of loss control. Good motivation can only be achieved over-all—it is unlikely that one can achieve it for loss control in isolation from the other activities of the firm.

In any event it is very unwise to rely on "missionary" type motivation. Effective loss control demands **control** measures to prevent certain events happening. This does not mean making regulations, it means enforcing them. If we do not have the means to enforce a loss control rule we need to alter our strategy to a more realisable programme.

"No smoking" notices are an attempt to enforce—not a statement of reality. If we want to make an area "no smoking" we need to take other action including:

1. control of matches and lighters (if justified and enforceable)

2. provision of safe "smoking" areas

3. action when smoking is discovered either directly or indirectly (presence of cigarette ends)

Chart 35 Active Loss Control shows some main points of training and motivation.

4.11 Human Safety

The Haddon strategy described earlier in this chapter (see Chart 27) was designed to deal with what he regarded as the epidemiological problem of road safety which each year kills and maims more people than most major wars have. It can be adapted to all industrial situations by considering the risk problems associated with "energy in the wrong place". We are particularly concerned with energy control, separation and protection.

As a start we can expand our previous approach on risk factors especially for activities and look for:—

— momentum e.g. speed/force of machinery/ transport

— height

— temperature

— pressure
— chemical
— radiation
— foreign object
— water

Our safety work should begin with analysis of the risk (thinking in energy terms in our normal operations and how it is handled. We should then determine the margin of safety against single and multiple failures. From this base modes of failure for non-standard operations can be reviewed. Finally we can prepare physical or system protection to handle foreseeable non-standard operations and modes of failure.

Our protection system and equipment must not depend on instruction, appeals to reason or virtue but be the means of building safety into the system. Protection will therefore result from normal human behaviour rather than be dependent on extra or special care. Chart 32 gives some risk factor specifics that can add directly or indirectly to danger or safety.

It is not possible to show individual safety methods and systems in detail in this book but Charts 33 and 34 give a short checklist of safety questions and a chart illustrating the risk management approach to human safety.

4.12 Property Loss Control

For each type of physical property risk we can produce an analysis of the physical exposure as a guide to specific control measures which should be the basis for systematic loss control as described earlier.

Typical charts for fire, explosion and theft are shown in Charts 37, 38 and 39. These are illustrative only and are not intended to be comprehensive. Having developed such a chart we can submit the proposed measures to further consideration for

1.   economy—as outlined in Chart 31.
2.   Training and motivation—as outlined in Chart 35.

For most industrial process situations much more detail will be needed and use may be made of mathematical models to explore various loss possibilities and to study the inter-relationship of the various factors.

ENERGY (mass/speed/height)

VOLUMES

SEPARATION

CODES

MARKINGS

PROCEDURES

INSTRUCTIONS

MOVING MACHINERY (energy)

UNNECESSARY OBJECTS AND WASTE (unnecessary energy for fire or collision)

STACKING (energy)

CHEMICALS

SPECIAL CIRCUMSTANCES

ORGANISATION (line management/safety adviser)

CHART 32—SOME RISK FACTOR SPECIFICS

1. Is this process/operation inherently safe?
    (i.e. no conceivable danger)
2. If not what does process/operation safety depend on?
3. Review effect of loss of each essential precaution?
4. Are the precautions realistic?
    a) do they interfere with the task (difficulty/access/speed)
    b) do they create discomfort
    c) are they otherwise limiting or unreasonable
5. Can the safety precautions
    a) fail accidentally?
    b) be sabotaged?
6. If so what would be the effect and how quickly?
    (is there reasonable time to recognise and respond?)
7. Does the job require unbalanced/unreasonable use of any limb or faculty?
8. Does the job require special dexterity or skill to maintain safety?
9. Is the working site accessible to anyone not directly involved?
10. If so in what circumstances and how could they be in danger?
11. Are there any opportunities or incitement for misuse of potentially dangerous equipment or facilities?
    (e.g. riding in hoists, playing with dangerous equipment)
12. Does safety depend on:
    a) observance of limits?
    b) correct coupling or mixture?
13. For 11 and 12 are there physical (preferably interlocking) controls to prevent misuse?

CHART 33—SOME SAFETY QUESTIONS

source of danger	specific origin	point of contact	control	standards	protection
HEAT	process accidental or deliberate fire	general	temperature	yes	shielding (including clothing cooling by water)
COLD	process	general	temperature	yes	clothing
OVERPRESSURE	explosion	general but especially torso	pressure control power tools	yes	pressure suits
UNDERPRESSURE	process e.g. diving compressed air				
FALLING OBJECTS	height (watch walls)	especially head and feet	weight height	no	safety helmets safety shoes
MOVING OBJECTS	exploding bottles	especially eyes	speed mass	no	shields, guards automatic cut off eye shields
CONTACT AT SPEED WITH FIXED OBJECTS	movement		speed mass	no	shields, guards
FALLING AND SMOTHERING	ladders powders, grains		height	yes	safety belt, harness note danger underneath
LIGHT	process	eyes		yes	eye shields
NOISE	process explosion	ears	loudness	yes	earmuffs
RADIATION	process	skin respiration	concentration	yes	shielding (including clothing)
POISONING — liquid — gas — solid	process	nose mouth skin	concentration	yes	masks, respirators, containment
OCCUPATIONAL DISEASE OR INJURY	overuse of limb overexposure			sometimes	

CHART 34—SAFETY ANALYSIS CHART

ACTIVE loss control

Some loss control measures are **passive** but they can be **affected by people.**

Other loss control measures are **active**—they require **action by people.**

Information

alert to loss potential

show possibility of prevention/reduction } use can be positive or negative

explain techniques

Training

acquire loss control skills

develop loss control competence } we can measure effect

overcome initial hesitancy

Motivation

create conditions to produce loss control response when needed

— recognition and control of hazards
— immediate correct response to loss event
— action to limit effect of loss

make it easy to be good—hard to be bad.

CHART 35—ACTIVE LOSS CONTROL

4.13 Earnings Loss Control

The risk in relation to earnings is any event inside or outside our organisation that will reduce our earnings significantly. In turn this usually means reduced volume of sales but could include increase in cost through necessary special steps to maintain production (the effect is the same —to reduce earnings). The impact on sales can come from a variety of sources, the most important being lack of production but we could lose sales as a result of loss of sales and other data, customer lack of confidence due to various events.

In order to protect earnings we need a clear picture of the exposure. The best method for analysing and understanding earnings dependencies is a flow chart tracing our products/services from key suppliers, through the various internal processes, the distribution network to final customers. We may have an important customer dependency on any single customer (or group of customers who could be affected by a single event) taking say more than 5% of sales.

A very simple chart is shown in Chart 36. Any real situation will produce a much more complex chart with perhaps 100 times as many items to be shown.

For suppliers we need to include all key utilities such as electricity, gas, water, drainage and labour. Sometimes we will need to take the supply chain back further than our immediate supplier.

Internally we need to treat each main process as a stage. Note we are looking at parallel processes in some cases, reducing the dependency. Separate buildings can usually be treated as separate risks and for some purposes different operations inside a single building can be treated as separate risks. (It will be realised that the size of exposure will vary considerably according to type of threat).

In assessing customer dependency we need to be on guard against any event that could involve several customers thus increasing the risk.

Chart 5 in Chapter II shows a simple chart for recording earnings exposures. In practice more detail will be needed and it will be helpful to add notes on special circumstances.

From such a table we can draw a contingency planning chart along the lines on Chart 40. Considerable practice will be needed before a detailed chart can be prepared without much re-drafting.

Once the chart is complete we need to add values exposed. We start on the right hand of the chart with a breakdown of all our earnings by the various customer segments (or if customer exposures are not very concentrated) by our various outputs.

The figures used should have two components:—

1. gross profit
2. associated overhead recovery (the amount allocated to the same and actual volume of sales that produce the gross profit)

Any event inside or outside the company that will reduce earnings significantly:

>   example

>>   reduced sales

>>   increased production costs

Sales may reduce due to physical hold up in production or supplies or:

>   lack of customer confidence

>   political reasons

>   sociological reasons

>   changes in fashion

To protect earnings it is important to have clear idea of exposure. Suggest use of flow chart to include:

— key suppliers

>   (all following factors to be considered for suppliers as well as self)

— utilities — electricity

>>   gas

>>   water

>>   drainage

>>   fuel

>>   labour

— key process areas

>   — machines

>   — operators

— internal processes

— packaging

— distribution

— key customers

CHART 36—EARNINGS RISK CONTROL

NOTE: (1) Fire needs ignition source, flammable material,
           oxygen, fire load to continue. We can control all four.

      (2) This note makes no special provision for arson.

PRE-EVENT   **Separation and reduced energy**

                 Ignition control
                    flameproof equipment
                    process enclosure
                    matches/lighters
                    review operating
                       temperatures/pressures and relieving
                          systems

                 Fire load control
                    reduce volume stored at one point
                    review materials used
                    separate storage and processes
                    limit storage areas

DURING EVENT   **Reduced energy and protection**
                 (limit oxygen and cost)

                 Detection system
                    smoke/heat detectors
                    fire alarm (needs manual intervention)
                 Fire fighting
                    manual — water/sand/foam
                           — extinguishers (correct type)
                           — hose reels
                    automatic — sprinklers
                              — deluge systems
                              — carbon dioxide/halon systems
                    removal of goods/equipment
                    smoke removal
                    protection against water

                 Review routes for growth of fire
                    fire doors
                    roofs
                    any connecting routes (permanent or
                       temporary)

POST EVENT   **Emergency treatment**

                    protect assets exposed to further damage

                 Contingency planning

                    alternative means of temporary production
                    steps to restore normal working

CHART 37—FIRE LOSS CONTROL

NOTE—see Chart 24 for conditions necessary for different types
of explosion.

PRE-EVENT   **Separation and reduced energy**

                   Ignition control
                       remove sources of ignition (flameproof,
                           matches, lighters)
                       process enclosure
                       keep atmosphere/operating conditions above
                           or below explosion envelope
                           (e.g. concentration of vapour gas)
                       remove dust
                       inerting

                   Explosion load control
                       reduce volume stored in area of danger
                       review materials used
                       separate storage and processes
                       limit storage areas
                       review operating temperatures/pressures
                       monitor corrosion and other deterioration
                           that could permit pressure burst

                   Reduced energy
                       relief systems for pressure vessels and all
                           enclosed (in buildings) operations

                   Protection
                       stronger walls, doors, roofs to prevent
                           interior damage (in nearby buildings)
                       blast walls etc.

                   Suppression systems
                       injection of gas, liquid, solid
                       shutting off of supply of flammable materials

DURING EVENT   **Reduced energy and protection**

                   Detection/Relieving systems
                       detectors
                       automatic warnings
                       relief valves/bursting discs
                       walls and roofs to relieve pressure

POST EVENT   **Emergency treatment**
                       protect assets exposed to further damage

                   Contingency planning
                       alternative means of temporary production
                       steps to restore normal working

CHART 38—EXPLOSION LOSS CONTROL

Uses techniques of other property loss control such as separation and protection but works by increasing energy requirement of thief in expectation of making risk trade-off for thief uneconomic. We are dealing with deliberate loss so denial of information is a control technique.

PRE-EVENT   **Separation, denial of information, increased energy**

Limit exposure
reduce amount/value stored at one place
location considerations
staff screening (if high risk)
staff motivation

Denial of information
limit notices and labelling to those essential for operational/safety reasons (but do not eliminate identification of goods which will facilitate recovery)
staff screening (if high risk)
control data outside organisation

Increased energy
locks
safes
location
security guards (balance against other risks)

DURING EVENT   **Protection, increased energy, denial of information**

Detection systems
photo-electric ⎫ watch trade-off for false
pressure ⎬ alarms and cost
window/door alarms

Security systems
verification of visitors/vehicles
separation
procedure changes (denial of information)

POST EVENT   **Emergency treatment**

protect assets exposed to further damage
review risk control systems (thieves and others have information)

Contingency planning
alternative means of temporary production
steps to restore normal working

CHART 39—THEFT LOSS CONTROL

AUTOMOTIVE CHEMICALS

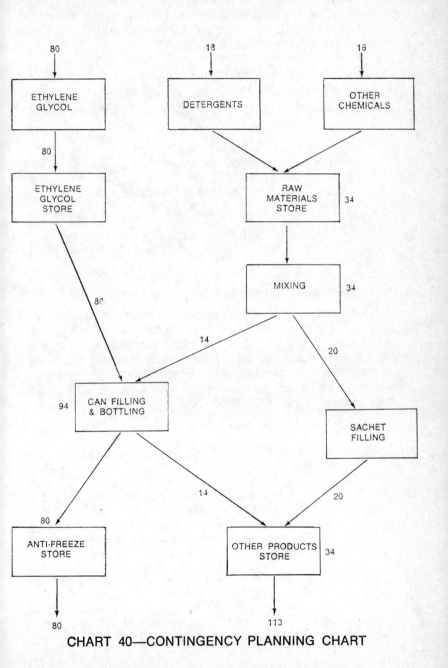

CHART 40—CONTINGENCY PLANNING CHART

Working backwards from right to left exposures are calculated for each operation or activity internal and external.
This will enable us to identify the key dependencies. One
other figure will need to be added—the likely cost of any
special expenses that could be involved in the loss of or
serious damage to each unit of plant.

When the information is complete on the chart, we can
consider possible steps to reduce the dependencies. These
can be divided into two broad categories:—

1.   Alterations in working procedures and operations
      now that will reduce the dependency (and alter the
      chart and the figures). These are improvements that
      could be made with advantage unrelated to any loss.

2.   Emergency procedures to be implemented after loss.

(In both cases we need to estimate the effect in cost and
benefit).

4.14   Contingency Planning

For simple activities the contingency planning exercise for
contingency planning can be prepared by a single risk
management specialist but for the typical industrial operation, it will be a major advantage to use a team principally
drawn from line management. Although at first sight this
seems to involve a great deal of effort, work will be saved
overall as:

1.   more ideas will be produced

2.   it will be possible to evaluate them critically at the
      same time

Contingency planning conferences can be very useful but
need careful preparation. By taking a team away for one or
more days attention can be focused on the problem and
as familiarity develops with each others problems the pace
of work increases.

We have found that a room with wallboards is very helpful.
The main activities chart can be displayed and other tables
put in front of participants. The use of a board to record all
suggestions helps to ensure that no idea is ignored whilst
permitting an orderly review of all alternatives.

4.15 Liability Loss Control

In previous chapters we have noted the main problems of liability risk:

1. It is everywhere—every employee's every action can have liability implications.
2. The exposure is not directly related to the culpability of the action. If a big loss results to someone else we may be liable.

Before considering liability loss control it may be helpful to restate in simple terms the basis of legal liability in order that we can plan effective economic practical control.

Chart 41 shows the spectrum of liability using the names commonly given to the different types of liability within the insurance industry.

SPECTRUM OF LIABILITY

Sources Contract — Statute — Custom

    Employers
    Occupier
    Carrier Note Differences
    Bailee
    Products
    Malpractice   ⎫ Note — Individual Duty of Care
                      ⎬   — Lack of Production/Design
    Professional Indemnity ⎭   Standards
    Public

All relate — To an Activity
           — To a Duty
           — To a Loss resulting from lack of compliance/lack of achievement

CHART 41

These various liabilities may be applied in different legal circumstances and Chart 42 illustrates in very simple form the main liability system—in a particular case we may be dealing with a hybrid liability situation.

LIABILITY SYSTEMS	CRITERIA	FACTORS
NEGLIGENCE (TORT)	CONDUCT OF DEFENDANT	PROBABILITY OF HARM SERIOUSNESS OF HARM PRECAUTIONS TAKEN
STRICT LIABILITY IMPLIED WARRANTY	QUALITY OF PRODUCT OR SERVICE	DEFECTIVE PRODUCT OR SERVICE DEFECT OF TIME PRODUCT LEFT DEFENDENT OF SERVICE DIRECTLY PROVIDED DEFECT CAUSED HARM
EXPRESS WARRANTY ABSOLUTE LIABILITY	SPECIFIC CONDITION(S)	CHECK AGAINST CONDITION(S)

CHART 42

Looking specifically at injury or death there are various heads of damage, some or all of which may be available in specific legal regions—Chart 43 illustrates.

HEADS OF DAMAGE

	MONETARY	NON-MONETARY
INJURED PERSON	LOSS OF EARNINGS EXTRA EXPENSE	PAIN & SUFFERING LOSS OF — EXPECTATION & LIFE — FACILITY
DEPENDANTS & OTHERS	SERVICES NEEDED FOLLOWING INJURY LOSS OF SUPPORT	LOSS OF SOCIETY

CHART 43

We summarise the elements of a liability loss in Chart 44 as a preliminary to considering the control problem.

LIABILITY RISK — THE PROBLEM
LIABILITY LOSS REQUIRES
    FAILURE TO CONFORM WITH LAW
        (PERFORM LEGAL DUTY)
    AS A RESULT OF FAILURE — HARM IS SUFFERED
        BY CONSUMER-USER
    LEGALLY ACCEPTABLE DEFENCE NOT AVAILABLE
THEREFORE WE NEED TO
    UNDERSTAND LAW
    OPERATE WITHIN THE LAW
    BE ABLE TO PROVE COMPLIANCE
LIABILITY CAN ARISE FROM
    COMMON LAW DUTY
    STATUTE LAW — SPECIFIC ACT OR REGULATION
    CONTRACT
BIGGEST PROBLEM
    ANY ACTION BY **ANY** EMPLOYEE
        CAN CREATE LIABILITY RISK
WE NEED
    RISK ANALYSIS
    TRAINING
    MOTIVATION
    ACTION AND REACTION

CHART 44

Liability loss control can be divided into several different stages:

1. running a good safe operation free from danger to employees, customers and others—either injury or loss.

2. ensuring that all employees understand the liability exposure and help to control it

3. reacting to all complaints from customers and others in such a way as to minimise the liability exposures

4. limited but effective use of legal defences

Chart 45 gives a simple checklist for Liability Risk Control.

It should be noted that we do not limit loss control to our own factories and network but seek to involve distributors, customers and others. Our labelling and instructions can teach and motivate if skilfully prepared. Warning notices can help others avoid risk and (provided they are part of an overall plan) limit our liability.

Employee understanding needs to be positive as well as negative. A negative approach might concentrate on denying responsibility, but this could be counter-productive if it annoyed a customer (leading to legal action) who could otherwise have been won over by sympathy.

Meeting reasonable claims quickly is not only good loss control by avoiding larger claims later but is good marketing in that it builds a good relationship between company and customer.

The legal situation is a system that can be understood and mastered. The first essential is to understand each party's attitude, strengths and weaknesses and then take a position that is reasonable as well as cost effective.

Note: Liability loss requires:
1. Failure to conform with/perform legal duty
2. As a result failure/harm is suffered by customer/employer third party
3. Legally acceptable defence not available

Therefore: We need to understand law
to operate within the law
be able to prove compliance

Our liability can arise:
1. From common law duty (Tort) e.g. negligence, assault, defamation
2. By statute law—specific act or regulation
3. By contract with other party

BIGGEST PROBLEM IS THAT ANY ACTION BY ANY EMPLOYEE CAN CREATE LIABILITY RISK

WE NEED: Risk analysis
Training
Motivation
Action and Reaction

PRE EVENT   Set up system of legal analysis and control
— understand current law
— have system for monitoring changes
— review contracts (standard and individual)
— training and advice for managers
— procedures for notification
Analyse purpose/use/possible misuse of our products/services
— design for safety
— safe production methods including training
— anticipate misuse/failure and consequences
— have system for feed-back on performance including failures and complaints
Control manufacture and use of product/service
— specification for production, distribution, training
— comply with appropriate codes (but do not rely on them)
— packaging to produce desired result
— labelling for safe use
— instructions in clear easy to understand language of user
— training for distributors/others as appropriate
— prevent unreasonable safety claims in advertising (implied and express)
Record so as to be able to prove innocence
— design
— production
— compliance with code etc.
— training results
— all warnings

DURING EVENT   Separate people/guards from danger
                — control of routing/walls/barriers
                — use of appropriate protection
                — procedures
                Train
                — distributors/staff/others to minimise danger and
                   react positively (including warning notices in
                   clear easy to use positions)
                Encourage
                — loss prevention (by example)
                — prompt disclosure of incidents that may result in
                   loss

AFTER EVENT   React positively
                — show concern and respond (not necessary to
                   admit liability)
                — can we satisfy complainant quickly and easily?
                — what can we learn from this incident?
                Establish legal countermeasures (if appropriate)
                — analyse attitude of plaintiff, lawyers/courts
                   (specifically — as it will effect us in this court
                   with these people at the likely date of trial)
                — prepare defence
                — make offer (if appropriate)
                Consider wider effect on business

CHART 45—LIABILITY RISK CONTROL

It is essential to remember that most liability claims escalate from small complaints as shown in the pyramid in Chart 46—note that in most cases the escalation is voluntary—we could prevent it.

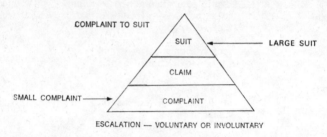

CHART 46

Chart 44 shows in slightly expanded form—the elements of successful legal defence of liability claims.

LEGAL DEFENCE STRATEGY

Legal Defence is part of overall Risk Control

Without waiting for an Action
    We Should

        1.   Assess Vulnerability
                (Product Stability)
                (Market Share)
                Technical Uncertainty
                Legal   ⎫
                Political ⎬
                Social   ⎭
                Competitor Competence
        2.   Arrange Legal Preparedness
                Legal Support
                  — Understanding
                Claims Involvement
                  — Insurer

CHART 47

4.16   Risk Transfer

The impact of risk on the company's assets and resources can be altered by risk transfer. It may be possible to make an outside party responsible for our loss by contract or non-contractual means. This can be achieved contractually by inserting a clause in the contract holding the other party responsible for our losses. This may be a very limited clause covering losses directly caused by the actions or negligence of the other party or it may be very wide. Obviously such clauses are a matter of both trade custom and negotiation — and the relative strength of the parties, especially in terms and need of services will help to determine the final outcome.

We may be required by contract to accept responsibility for the losses of others, either caused by our own action or on a wider basis.

Outside of the strict contractual situation, we may have legal obligations or other parties may have legal obligations to us, both of which involve some transfer of risk.

When considering our obligations to others we need to take a very broad view for risk control purposes even though we may be confident that we can avoid legal responsibility. When we review the liability of others to us it may seem at first sight that we have an effective means of transferring the cost of risk through the operations of their legal liability.

Although the other party may appear to be liable at law we may still fail to recover. They may successfully dispute our claim in the courts, or they may be "men of straw" with no financial resources to meet their obligations.

Great attention has been paid in the past to the use of risk transfer methods through the use of "hold harmless" and other clauses that imposed or avoided burdens. There is an increasing tendency for such clauses to be set aside in court, especially where the operation of the clause would be unreasonable. Despite this reducing effectiveness of risk transfer it is most important that:—

1. The risk arising under common and statute law and contract are clearly understood.

2. Risk transfer by contract is used where appropriate although undue reliance should not be placed on risk transfer to give adequate risk control.

Chapter V

Risk Financing

5.1 The Risk Financing Problem

If one views risk as future uncertainty, then risk financing must be the financing of any short-fall in our expected future assets and earnings resulting from the impact of uncertainty. This risk financing need can arise in many different ways. It may result from the regular and almost continuous impact of risk on a number of the commercial activities of the firm, such as breakages of glass or motor vehicle accidental damage, or small thefts. If the cost of such losses can be calculated in advance it will be possible to allow for them in budgetary systems, so that they become a regular on-cost of the business.

Another type of risk financing may result from the need to rebuild a factory after loss. Here the probability of the loss of a factory by, say, fire is quite small, and the mechanism of insurance usually provides a convenient means of transferring the risk financing problem. For a small premium, payable now, one is given the facility of sufficient finance (within the terms of the insurance policy arranged) to rebuild the factory after loss. Similar insurance solutions for low probability situations are available for financing, again within policy limits; the financial impact of business interruption resulting from fire and other stated perils, or the depletion of assets resulting from legal action by third parties.

Yet another risk financing need arises from non-insurable events that cause a depletion of assets and earnings. These include the last six categories of loss shown under Chart 1 in Chapter I, losses resulting from management, from wastage, from technological causes, from social reasons, from political causes and from the physical environment.

The normal method used by management to cope with the uncertainties of such events is to make sure that adequate finance is available to preserve the viability of the enterprise in these contingent situations. If one of these causes results in a sharp loss of sales, one needs to have enough finance to meet overheads and other fixed costs until either the market changes, or one is able successfully to redeploy the assets previously locked up in the business. One of the most important skills for the management of a business is to balance the need for prudence in terms of available resources in the event of contingencies with the additional profit or return available from redeployment of those resources. In recent years we have seen a number of quite large businesses fail because their management had not taken into account the possibility of such big and sudden changes as subsequently occurred in the markets in which they operated.

At this stage one should remark that risk does not always result in loss. It may result in gain. For commercial risk, the whole objective behind the taking of risk is indeed to achieve a gain in net assets and an improvement in earnings. The possibility of this gain arises because by taking the risk one will be able to achieve a return on capital greater than the cost of the capital. It further arises because one has correctly anticipated a need of one's fellow men and women, a need for which they are willing to pay a price that reflects the cost of meeting that need, and the risk taken by committing resources in advance of the manifestation of their needs in the shape of a purchase or commitment to purchase on their part.

For some businesses the risk is quite small because the commitment of assets is quite small. This situation can arise even where quite large assets are used in the business if they are used in such a way that there is considerable flexibility for their redeployment in the event of the expected course of events not producing the expected return. Such businesses have a high service component and a low risk component. For most businesses, however, managing risk is a central part of their overall work and the achievement of reasonable profitability depends on the anticipation and management of risk situations.

If we examine the possible range of financial outcomes from a specific operation over a specific period, we can see the variation in outcome in terms of total possible loss or total possible gain, with the expected outcome being somewhere between these two extremes. If we can assess the likely outcome with confidence we can similarly assess the extent to which this likely outcome will give us a return for the taking of risk that is above the return we could get from the commitment of our resources to a safe activity.

5.2 Methods of Financing Risk

There are many methods of financing risk and among the most important are:

(1) Operating budgets.
(2) Special internal funds.
(3) Special external grants.
(4) Credit.
(5) Insurance.

We can evaluate the advantages and disadvantages of each method by consideration of the effect on cash flow, taxation, earnings, share price and market standing and position.

5.3 Operating Budgets

Meeting losses out of operating budgets has the advantage of eliminating unnecessary cost, such as insurers' expenses and profits. Money expended in this way is not spent until it is needed to pay for a loss, whereas insurance premiums are paid at the beginning of a period of insurance.

The more important advantage of this method of financing is that it becomes possible to monitor loss control performance in the same way as any other budgetary performance. This can have an important psychological impact on the frequency and extent of losses, as the situation of "don't worry its insured" is replaced by a situation where local management is held accountable for the success or failure of its risk control activity.

The financing of risk from operating budgets is usually only appropriate for the relatively small and predictable losses that regularly occur, as with this method the cash needs are regular and predictable. For a medium-sized company, the amount of insurance premium expended on this type of risk can be considerable and will possibly exceed 50% of the total premiums. Practical difficulty will normally be experienced in obtaining the right discount from insurers when a policyholder decides to retain for himself a stated first amount of each loss. The method normally used by insurers to calculate such discounts is to examine the number of losses of this category that have occurred over the previous year or years, allow for their on-costs and make a percentage reduction. The main disadvantage of this method is that it would give a higher discount to the poorly-managed firm than to the well managed one, so that any inaccuracy in original rating is magnified by the application of discounts.

5.4   Internal Funds

Where a financing need is less predictable and of greater potential size, recourse may be had to special internal funds. Companies use funds to meet all types of financing needs, such as replacing equipment or tax equalisation. The object of such a fund is to accumulate finance to meet a special and expected need. A self insurance fund can be used to build up resources so that more risk can be retained. It is appropriate for the risk that is too big to retain and meet out of local operating budgets. Sometimes a company will establish or augment such funds in years when its profits or earnings performance is good with the implication that the fund will not be used for losses occurring in high profit years but will be used to supplement otherwise meagre profits by loss payments in more difficult years. Use of a fund in this way exactly mirrors the use of such internal funds for tax equalisation and equipment replacement.

One of the disadvantages of self-insurance funds in most countries is that they are not tax-deductible whereas insurance premiums usually are. Losses occurring within the financial year can, of course, usually be offset for tax purposes in that year, but there is no way in most countries where a company can fund for future losses from untaxed revenue sources. The internal fund used for year-to-year loss funding must, therefore, be established either from capital sources or from revenue sources that have borne tax. This inability to fund without tax penalty is one of the reasons why large numbers of major companies have formed their own "captive" insurance companies.

5.5   External Grants

Debate rages on the ethics and logic of companies relying on special external grants to meet their risk financing needs. The years since the last World War have seen a growth in special payments to business enterprises to protect them and their employees and customers against the effects of sudden loss.

Although the various government catastrophe schemes for relief after disaster often distinguish between private and business property, there is usually some degree of provision for business losses to be met out of public funds. It might, therefore, seem appropriate for companies when considering the risk financing needs following a natural disaster to take into account, at least to some extent, the likelihood and character of government aid.

We might even extend this principle to commercial risk as recent years have provided a number of examples of governments "bailing out" large companies that have got into financial trouble. Such government help is usually given on the basis that the concern in question is vital to the national economy and interest, particularly if it is important for employment.

There is room for debate on the reliability of such government aid to cope with the disaster that has not yet occurred and there may be some question of the moral issues involved in relying for help from public funds, but the trend is there for all to see.

5.6 Credit for Risk Financing

The use of credit for risk financing has varied in recent times. For insurable events occasional use has been made of what is called contingent credit, a form of "stand-by" credit which will be made available on pre-determined terms if a specified contingent event occurs. Several years ago the use of contingent credit to provide finance for future losses was generally accepted in the financial market, and finance could be made available on a payment of an annual fee of between $\frac{1}{8}$% and 2%. Where high insurance rates were involved and the event seemed of low probability relatively cheap contingent credit appeared to provide a good alternative to insurance.

In recent years, however, bankers have begun to realise that in many respects contingent credit was last resort credit, particularly as the payment of the annual commitment fee still left the company in the position of paying, after loss, substantial rates of interest. Whilst these rates of interest looked adequate by normal commercial standards, they would be below the rates which a banker would charge for credit of last resort. Once the matter was studied it became obvious that in good years, companies would not make use of the credit line which they did not need, but in difficult times this particular line of credit following loss would become a most desirable asset of the borrowing company.

For commercial risk the use of credit is normal and acceptable. The practical problem for most companies is that once the difficult commercial situation arises, the reduction in their likely future assets makes the securing of additional loan finance on reasonable terms difficult, if not impossible. The correct strategy must, therefore, be to endeavour to anticipate the range of outcomes that is likely and to make sure that a financial solution is available for each of these outcomes. It will be appreciated that a high flow of profit may only cause temporary financing problems, such as the expansion of raw material and processing costs such as work in progress but the failure of the market to meet expectations in terms of sales will cause more serious problems. In practice, the company's risk situation will often fluctuate quite sharply, and for a company in difficulties there may be no alternative to taking some more, and perhaps unreasonable, risk other than to wind the company up before the expected unpleasant eventuality occurs.

5.7   Insurance as a Method of Financing Risk

For non-commercial risk the most widely used form of risk financing is, of course, insurance. We should not forget the valuable service that the insurance market provides for the business man in enabling him to deal with the financing needs of a large range of unscheduled and undesirable events. The ability to replace such possible losses by a certain, and much smaller, expenditure in the form of a premium has always appeared to most business men as a valuable risk trade off facility.

There is a tremendous attraction for the business man faced by risk and uncertainty in all directions to welcome the capability to remove a whole range of uncertainties for what appears to be a relatively small premium. The purchase of insurance remains one of the most important risk financing decisions. Such buying decisions should be taken after first determining the risk financing need and then evaluating the insurance alternatives, but all too often the insurance buying decision is taken, either on the basis of tradition or from the relatively limited range of insurance solutions that seem to be available.

5.8 Evaluating Alternative Methods of Financing

In evaluating the alternatives for insurable risk we need to take into account a number of factors including:

— **Cover.** The range of unscheduled and undesirable events for which risk financing is provided by means of insurance together with consideration of the circumstances in which such protection is made available.

— **Limits.** The extent of insurance cover made available in financial terms, either expressed as a sum insured or a limit of liability.

— **Premium.** The price to be paid for this cover within these limits as an insurance premium.

— **Cash Flow.** The payment terms, including considerations of instalments and due dates.

— **Stability of rate.** Is the rate of premium being quoted a realistic one in the light of the likely loss pattern or is it an artificially low rate quoted as an inducement to transfer the business? It may not be wrong to accept such an artificially low rate but if it is accepted one should be mindful of the risk that next year one may have to pay more premium as a result of the unreality of today's rate.

— **Liability.** The solvency of the insurer both in the short and the long term. Here regard should be paid to the likely pattern of claims payments. When we are considering fire or other property insurance, the claims need will be relatively prompt but in other areas, such as substantial third party liability and marine hull claims, a considerable delay in payment may be the normal pattern and here we need to make sure that our proposed insurance looks safe over the time span of the claims need.

— **Services.** The services connected with insurance which are needed should be considered as well as the services available.

— **Method.** The method of insurance involved; for example, whether to buy direct or to use the services of an insurance broker, should be considered.

It is very important when buying insurance to check policy wordings. Most of the terms and conditions in an insurance policy have the effect of limiting cover and have been introduced because of the impact of a particular claim or claims in the past.

It should also be remembered that the risk financing need is continually changing and it will be necessary to monitor that risk financing need as well as the performance of the insurers and insurance brokers.

5.9 Evaluation of Insurance Cover

Chart 48 gives in summary form the range of insurances available today in most insurance markets. The table is by no means comprehensive but is intended to give a broad picture and may be used in conjunction with Chart 1 which gave a similar broad classification of threats to the business enterprise. As this is not a text book on insurance, we will not examine the classes of insurance but limit our consideration to methods of evaluating insurance cover.

PROPERTY

    FIRE can include explosion, lightning, earthquake, storm, malicious damage, etc., impact by vehicle or aircraft   Sum Insured related to value

    ALL RISKS on specified items

    GOODS IN TRANSIT
    LIVESTOCK
    COMPUTER
    BOILER & MACHINERY—inspection
    MONEY
    VALUABLE DOCUMENTS

PEOPLE

    LIFE—individual or group
    PERSONAL ACCIDENT   Specified (accepted) sums to be paid in event of death or specified injury

EARNINGS

    LOSS OF PROFITS
    NON-RECOVERY OF OVERHEADS
    ADDITIONAL EXPENSES   Formula to calculate actual loss

    Computer
    Livestock
    Research
    Advanced profits
    Loss of Book Debts

LIABILITIES
  Employers Liability
  Public Liability—to third parties
  Product Liability—for goods or services. Usually limited
                      to property loss or damage and personal injury.

Many special liability policies include:—
  Libel and Slander
  Pollution
  Patent Suit/Trademark Infringement
  Restrictive Covenant.

MOTOR POLICY can include
PROPERTY
  ACCIDENTAL DAMAGE as specified—basis of payment is actual
                          up to limit of market value
                          (or agreed value) of vehicle

  LIABILITY to third parties includes legal cost of defence
    —unlimited for private vehicles but specified limit for commercial
    vehicles
  Additionally private motor car insurance may include:—
    — loss of personal effects in vehicle
    — loss of garage by fire, etc.
    — personal accident insurance

MARINE

HULL POLICY covers—total loss/accidental damage by stated
                    (marine) perils
                    —75% liability for collision damage
                    salvage and other special charges

  Separate WAR POLICY covers mines and other war risks
  PROTECTION AND INDEMNITY POLICY covers other 25% collision
    liability and other specified liabilities of shipowner

AVIATION
  Usually combined policy for (1) HULL RISKS
                          (2) LIABILITY to third parties, (inc.
                                      passengers)

TRANSPORT OF GOODS
  Goods-in-transit policy for land risks
            Cargo Policy can cover shipment by land sea and air.

CHART 48—A CLASSIFICATION OF U.K. INSURANCE
    POLICIES   (N.B. This is not a complete list)

The biggest practical difficulty facing the unskilled (and
often the skilled) insurance buyer is the complexity of
policy wordings and terms and conditions. Often the buyer
gives up the comparison task as hopeless and relies on
a single criterion, that of premium, to evaluate different
insurance offers.

Where one is dealing with an irregular and infrequent event the dangers of this system will not be apparent until the large claim occurs that is found to be uninsured, and which shows that, in fact, in comparing covers and deciding on the basis of price alone, one was not comparing like with like.

The best method of comparison is to list each of the main conditions found in the policies to be compared in tabular form so that one can see at a glance precisely what each cover offers. This may be a quite lengthy process and for the more complex policy wordings will seem at first sight a most difficult proceeding.

If the sum of premium is not large one can limit the table of comparisons to the more important features, but where one is dealing with the insurance of a valuable factory it is most important to compare all the available terms. Such comparison should not be limited to the cover provided by several different alternative insurances but the cover offered should also be compared with the risk needs as found and established by the risk identification process described in Chapter II.

5.10 Insurable Values and Limits of Liability

When buying insurance for an item of property one needs to calculate the future rebuilding or re-equipment price of the property insured in order to provide an effective financing solution. In order to provide an accurate answer, one needs to ask a number of questions including:—

1. What production capacity will be needed to provide the same earnings pattern? At the moment the factory might be too big for likely future needs and it would be necessary to determine to what extent we would have to cover this excess value in the factory. It might be a requirement of a loan covering the factory, for example, that it is fully insured. In other cases it might be impossible to provide a new factory to give the necessary production capacity at the estimated current value of our present factory.

2. What new legal and other requirements will a new factory face compared with the existing plant? In most parts of the world it is impossible to rebuild a factory today in the same form as the present factory was built some years ago. Additional safety and anti-pollution requirements will usually require a more complex

plant and often management will wish to take advantage of the change to build a plant that contains, for example, more monitoring equipment.

3. How long would it take to rebuild the factory, assuming that the loss took place on the last day of the insurance policy?

4. What possible delays and dependencies are crucial as regards building and equipping the new factory?

5. What would be the market effects of the loss? Could it result in substantial interruption of earnings and could the non-availability of our production result in permanent market changes?

6. What foreign currency problems will arise, such as the purchase of plant overseas? The changing pattern of rates of exchange in recent years has meant many problems for companies needing to replace equipment bought from overseas countries with currencies at much higher values.

7. What are the main tax considerations, and how confident are we that the present tax arrangements will continue into the future? Sometimes the effect of tax will reduce the post-financing need, but there is always the possibility of a change in taxation between the time the insurance is arranged and the time of loss, resulting in a risk financing deficit after the loss.

8. What would be the effects of obsolescence and change over the period covered by the insurance and the rebuilding time at the factory?

Similar considerations apply in the consideration of limits for the purposes of liability insurance. One needs to take into account the change in the legal situation not only over the period of insurance covered by the policy but over the period which it might take for an action brought by a claimant to come to court. This means, therefore, considering, in some countries, the impact of legal change over six or more years. In assessing likely insurance needs one must take into account not only changes in the law but changes in the manner and the extent to which the law is applied. One may be faced with a situation where the law does not change but changing social and political factors are reflected in differing legal attitudes, so that a greater loss is suffered than had been anticipated.

Consideration may be given to limitation of liability by statutory means in a number of situations such as those of collisions at sea and in many ports and harbours of the world. Sometimes similar limitation is embodied in statutes covering accidents on land. Any change in liability will usually be easily discoverable and additional insurance can be taken out, but an alteration in the conditions of enforcement of law which could result from a single legal decision, is not discoverable in advance. Nevertheless possible changes need to be anticipated if at all possible.

When considering liability limits, one should remember that in the absence of contractual limitation of liability, the potential exposure of the company is often its total assets. It is certainly the case that the larger and more well known the company, the more it is at risk from legal action, as plaintiffs and their legal advisers recognise the availability of assets and the vulnerability of the company's reputation.

For many small businesses insurance to full liability limits is financially impossible, and the normal course adopted is to insure to a reasonable limit and then to accept that in the event of the very remote liability situation resulting in catastrophic loss the company may be forced to go out of business.

While the ultimate extent of liability may be the full assets of the company concerned, there will be many activities where a medium-sized firm could be severely jeopardised, such as when, as a result of some contracting activity, without limitation of liability, it brings about the loss of valuable property such as a number of ships or aircraft or a major factory. Practical financing considerations will dictate the need to assess as a trade-off the balance between buying additional cover and avoiding unnecessary exposure. Where the activity being undertaken is potentially hazardous and large losses could result it is usually preferable to buy more cover at the top end, where it is relatively cheap, even at the risk of accepting as uninsured some of the loss at the bottom end.

5.11 Comparison of Insurance Premium and Cash Flow

Although a great deal of mystique attaches to insurance, once an evaluation of cover and limits has been made, any evaluation of premium payments should be made in exactly the same way as any other financing evaluation. One should, for example, calculate the future cost of any premium instalments in terms of today's present value, using the appropriate interest rate for discounting purposes.

Bearing in mind the time span involved in settling many liability claims, it is important to relate the premium paid to Insurers at inception of a policy to the outflow of cash in the form of claims payment by Insurers. As this may take place over 5 to 10 years, the investment income gain by the Insurers whilst they retain premiums pending claims settlements can often exceed the premium originally paid to them.

To illustrate this an example of a liability insurance which produces a loss ratio of 100% on net premiums to the Insurers, will in fact produce a good profit if cash flow is taken into account.

Example (this is over simplified to clearly explain concept)

Liability Insurance Premium £100,000
Claims   £100,000

Claims settlement pattern

10% in year 1
20% in year 2
40% in year 3
60% in year 4
80% in year 5
90% in year 6
95% in year 7
100% in year 8

Year 1	Premium	£100,000	
	Claims	10,000	
	Surplus	£ 90,000	
	Investment income at 10%		9,000
Year 2	Surplus	90,000	
	Claims	10,000	
		80,000	
	Investment income at 10%		8,000
Year 3	Surplus	80,000	
	Claims	20,000	
		60,000	
	Investment income at 10%		6,000

Year 4	Surplus	£ 60,000	
	Claims	20,000	
		40,000	
	Investment income at 10%		4,000
Year 5	Surplus	40,000	
	Claims	20,000	
		20,000	
	Investment income at 10%		2,000
Year 6	Surplus	20,000	
	Claims	10,000	
		10,000	
	Investment income at 10%		1,000
Year 7	Surplus	10,000	
	Claims	5,000	
		5,000	
	Investment income at 10%		500
Year 8	Surplus	5,000	
	Claims	5,000	
		NIL	

Total investment income	£30,500
Original premium	£100,000
	£130,500

Actual loss ratio = 76.6%   (100,000) (claims)

(130,500) Premium/
Investment)

In order to enable the Insured to participate in the investment income and relate premium payments more directly to claims settlement, many insurers have introduced retrospecting rating schemes, which are particularly suitable for liability insurances.

The following example provides the investment income sharing concept with protection for the Insured against wild claim fluctuations during the period of insurance.

KEY

A = Deposit premium based on the anticipated total premium under normal rating methods

B = Payment to Insurers for normal expenses

C = Cost of settled and outstanding claims

D = Specific claims handling expenses

X = Loss conversion factor which provides for normal claims expenses and profit

Y = Minimum premium payable

Z = Maximum premium payable

The retrospective premium would be calculated as follows if we assume a loss conversation factor of 15%.

Premium

A =	20% of 1,000,000	=£200,000
B =	Expenses say 5%	50,000
		£250,000 Deposit

Claims

C =	£500,000	500,000
D =	£ 50,000	50,000
		£550,000
X =	Conversion factor of 15%	£550,000 x 1.15
		£632,500

Balance due to Insurers = £632,500 minus £250,000

= £382,500

If the balance of the premium is paid as claims are settled the cash benefit to the Insured can be significant.

It is often typical to have protection against the fluctuation of large claims by having a minimum premium of 50% of the anticipated premium (A x 2.5) and a maximum of 150% of the anticipated premium (A x 7.5). In addition there might also be an individual loss limitation of say £100,000 per occurrence, the cost of which is included in the loss conversion factor. The retrospective premium calculation is therefore:—

1.15 $(C + D) - (A + B)$

Minimum premium $A \times 2.5 = B$

Maximum premium $A \times 7.5 = B$

Methods of retrospective rating are numerous. Each needs very careful analysis and relation to the class of business, the claim settlement pattern and the maximum exposure. The principles should be:

— Low deposit premium

— Additional payment as claims are settled by Insurers

— Protection against impact on rating plan of large claims or significant accumulation of small claims.

5.12 Stability of Rate

The stability of premium is a factor usually overlooked by insurance buyers, or at least not fully taken into account. Many insurance premium rates appear ridiculously low and, indeed, if one were to calculate the present risk they would be ridiculously low. In these cases one is faced with a bargain in insurance buying, but it is important to bear in mind that, following loss, not only will this bargain cease to be available from the present insurers, but other insurers will have been alerted to the possibilities of loss if the incident causing loss is sufficiently well known. There is a trend amongst the bigger buyers to regard stability of premium as at least as important as premium cost itself. Where management is concerned with planning a long-term project and insurance costs are high, as in the case of aircraft or ships, a stable insurance premium is a necessity in making the overall investment decision.

The failure of a number of insurance companies in different parts of the world in recent years has caused more attention to be paid to the solvency of insurers. It is difficult for the average buyer to evaluate solvency directly and although in some countries guides are provided to the solvency of the insurers, these only assess the present situation and cannot take into account a deterioration in the insurer's position due to imprudent underwriting or reinsurance, or the solvency of the company's reinsurers.

5.13 Insurance Services and Insurance Brokers

The use and quality of services provided by insurance brokers varies substantially between insurance markets.

Some insurance markets have little or no broking capability on offer. In other cases the industrial market in particular is largely organised by insurance brokers. Most markets have a mixture of buyers or other intermediaries. A large company will often buy part of its insurance direct and use insurance brokers for other parts.

When considering how to improve insurance buying within an industrial group one needs to assess the work of broking services in terms of their effect on the management of the risk exposure. Brokerage expenditure can be justified if it:

1. helps to ensure that the risk exposures are properly handled by insurance and non-insurance measures;

2. results in more effective buying than the company could arrange direct with the insurers;

3. helps to reduce the insured and non-insured losses of the company;

4. has the overall effect of improving the financial performance of the company by reducing expenditure and avoiding losses.

A good professional insurance broker should undertake the following services as required by his clients:

1. Familiarise himself completely with the client's operations, so as to be able to review the property, earnings and liability exposures of the client thoroughly.

2. Prepare, in conjunction with the client, a plan for handling such exposures, including the buying of insurance.

3. Calculate, together with the client's financial staff, a suitable level of risk retention.

4. Advise the client on all types of property, earnings and liability loss prevention and, where appropriate, assist in implementation.

5. Buy insurance on behalf of his client, having regard to the cover needed, the level of premium required, the services to be provided by insurers, including inspection, survey, documentation and claims, and the solvency and stability of the insurer.

6. In most circumstances, handle claims and negotiate both settlements and recoveries.

In providing these services the broker needs to deploy a wide range of technical staff. A comprehensive review of the exposures of an industrial concern requires a great deal of information and the broker will need to work with various key personnel of his client. The broker's ability to buy effectively depends on the quality of his staff, the volume or weight of his account, the skill of his brokers in buying and the technical thoroughness of his submissions to insurers.

There are many exposure situations where available insurance policy wordings do not meet the particular needs of the client. The good broker is able to suggest innovations in these circumstances, matching his special knowledge of the client's needs to his appreciation of what the insurers are willing to offer. Many new policy forms and endorsements originate with brokers' submissions to insurers.

In serving the large client, the broker should be able to use world-wide markets to meet specific insurance needs, and it is important that he is fully acquainted, by direct and correspondent contact, with conditions in all the major insurance markets. A good network of subsidiaries and correspondents makes it possible to advise and help on local problems of the client overseas. The broker's knowledge of market should help him to anticipate trends and guide his client accordingly and his advice should be based on trends, as well as present day situations.

Sometimes the client may feel that he does not require the assistance of a broker in assessing or helping to assess the exposures in his business and working out a plan to deal with them. In these circumstances, if he employs a broker at all, the broker's role may well be limited to the purchase of insurance. Even in this limited situation, however, the broker's position in law, when acting for his client in the purchase of insurance, requires the full disclosure of relevant information and the task of assimilating all the information required may still be a considerable one.

The broker normally receives his remuneration as commission on premiums expended by the insured and an unfortunate consequence of this situation is that the more premium a client pays the higher is the broker's income. This presents some difficulty in a situation where the best advice to a large client is to retain many of the risks himself, thus reducing the broker's income. Although most of the larger brokers now undertake a certain volume of fee work, the bulk of their income still arises from commission on insurances purchased on behalf of their clients. As this commission only arises from the client's decision to purchase, it should be regarded as under the client's control in the same way as the fees paid to other professional buyers, such as solicitors and accountants. Already a number of corporations throughout the world require from their brokers a statement of income earned on their account, thus putting themselves in a position to discuss with the brokers the adequacy of their commission income in relation to services provided. It is only reasonable to add that a large professional broker has to maintain extensive advisory services which are used partly on each of his major accounts, but cannot easily be directly allocated to one particular account in whole or part.

5.14 Self-Insurance

There has been considerable debate as to whether there is such a thing as "self-insurance". It used to be argued that self-insurance was nothing more than non-insurance— i.e. failure to insure. During the past few years it has begun to be accepted that self-insurance applies to a conscious decision not to insure when the circumstances of risk reproduce inside an industrial company or other enterprise most or the normal conditions of the insurance process, mainly that there is some spread of risk and some predictability in the pattern of loss.

Where there is sufficient spread of loss, sufficient regularity of occurrence of loss and one can predict the extent of loss with some confidence, then we are only concerned with the company's capability to finance the loss. Where the losses are regular and semi-predictable we can be certain that the insurance premium already takes into account or will shortly take into account, the cost of such losses plus the insurer's expenses in handling, plus the insurer's expected profit. In these circumstances self-insurance through operating budgets or internal funding will almost certainly result in considerable economies compared with the insurance method.

There are practical limits to the amount of self-insurance that can economically be undertaken. As the scale of loss rises and the possibility of loss reduces, the trade off from self-insurance becomes more uncertain and the insurance method appears the most advantageous. For a large company with substantial spread of risk it is often possible to produce a fail-safe situation where, as a result of self-insurance, there is a certainty of saving money, if the losses to be absorbed are compared with the reduction in insurance premium. By "fail-safe" we mean that the worst result to be experienced with a new self-insurance scheme will still leave the company better off in financial terms than it would otherwise be. This fail-safe limit falls well below the point at which most industrial companies could assume all of their risk, so there remains a substantial need for insurance. The fail-safe solution implies that the premium saving will be bigger than the losses retained, but some companies have found it advantageous to consider risk retention in situations where there was a strong possibility, but no certainty, that risk retention would be profitable.

5.15   Risk Retention Limits

In considering the extent of risk retention, one can always afford to expose up to the limit of the premium saved if one is confident that the losses will not exceed this figure. When one extends the loss exposure, in probable terms above this figure, a limit needs to be put upon such risk retention to avoid unnecessary strain on the company's earnings and liquidity. As far as earnings are concerned, most financial directors think in terms of retaining no more risk than will be covered by a 1% shortfall in earnings, it being felt that this is the maximum deflection acceptable to the company as a result of more risk retention. The formula of all premium savings, plus 1% of earnings before tax, is being more widely accepted as a basis for limiting self-insurance premiums.

In many countries the capability of a large company to retain the occasional loss that is within its capacity to bear is not matched by a willingness on the part of regular insurance market to give appropriate discounts. In these circumstances, one either needs the help of a skilled professional adviser to re-negotiate the rearranged insurance buying, or one should consider whether the company is large enough to form a captive insurance company, which accepts, either directly or by reinsurance, the risks of the company, using the reinsurance market to limit the captive company's exposure to an amount appropriate to the financial resources of the parent. Before considering captive insurance companies further, it should be stated that self-insurance can have an important psychological advantage in removing the feeling of "don't worry—it's insured". If uninsured losses

are treated as a controlled cost, substantial improvement
in loss performance is usually possible.

5.16 Captive Insurance Companies

A captive insurance company is an insurance company
formed by an industrial or commercial group to insure all
or part of the risks of its parent. Such companies are not
new, many having been formed in the last century. In fact
many of today's prominent normal insurers began as captive insurance companies, formed by their parents, because
their needs in terms of either cover or price were not being
met by the normal insurance market.

The main advantage of a captive insurance company lies
in the tax deductability of insurance premiums and premium
funds compared with the normal self-insurance. In fact, there
are two main tax reasons for the formation of an insurance
company by an industrial group to handle all or part of its
own insurances. First, any funding for self-insurance future
losses without the use of an insurance company involves
building up a fund from capital or taxed revenue sources
(the position varies between different countries and in some
countries, notably Holland, self-insurance funds are partially
relieved from tax). By contrast, premiums paid to an insurance company will normally be tax deductible and within
limits which vary from country to country these premiums
may be retained for varying periods of time within the premium funds of the insurance company without being given
into consideration for tax purposes. In brief, there is a
penalty for the self insurer who does not have his own
insurance company. The second reason for tax minimisa-
tion is concerned with the operation of captive insurance
companies offshore. In Bermuda "exempt" insurance companies currently only pay a flat tax of BD$2,000 per annum.
If such a captive insurance company retained its earnings
it can build up its premium funds and capital very quickly
indeed.

For British-owned companies the location of insurance
companies offshore was limited by Bank of England control to Sterling Area countries only. As a result the most
popular location for British companies in recent years has
been the island of Guernsey in the Channel Islands. Here
there were two alternative means of forming insurance companies. The first involved the use of a "corporation tax"
company with a flat rate tax per annum of £300. In this case
the word "insurance" could not be used in the title of the

company and the management of the company had to be conducted offshore from Guernsey (and to maintain the tax advantage this meant a location where management is not subject to a higher tax). This method is no longer allowed by the authorities. The alternative method of forming captive insurance companies in Guernsey involves location on the island, paying normal tax of 20% and obtaining permission for the use of the word "insurance" in the title from the States Advisory and Finance Committee. In order to secure such permission it is necessary to submit a fairly detailed application and reasonably substantial capitalisation is normally required.

Captive insurance companies can be formed in most of the major industrialised countries, although in most cases the formation of any insurance company involves substantial documentation and delay. Apart from Bermuda and Guernsey, a number of other locations are favourable for the formation of insurance companies including Curaçao, the Cayman Islands, Hong Hong and the Bahamas.

In most respects the operation and management of captive insurance companies is similar to that of a normal insurance company. Their operational needs can be considered under the headings of legal documentation, accounting and taxation, underwriting, claims handling, investment, reinsurance, administration and loss control.

The legal requirements of insurance companies are more complex than those of normal companies. When a large industrial group forms a captive insurance company it will be necessary to take account of local law in the country of formation and obviously one would try and ensure compliance with the group's own legal procedures. In every country there are special requirements for the formation of insurance companies which must be complied with.

In most countries governments have established insurance supervisory bodies that exercise fairly detailed legislative control over insurance companies. The requirements are complex and usually include minimum capitalisation, separation of premium funds, limitation on investment and control of type of investment, sometimes approval of management, and inevitably a requirement for regular detailed operating returns. Apart from ensuring compliance with such legislation when the new company is formed, it will be necessary to establish a monitoring system to keep up to date with many changes that are made in insurance regulations.

For the executive who has been concerned with insurance operations in one country only, the establishment of captive insurance companies elsewhere may reveal a host of new problems, including detailed licensing of insurance by class and policy and controls on the insurance overseas or "non-admitted" insurance. As a result, many recent captives limit their direct acceptances to one country only and participate in the rest of their company's overseas insurance by means of reinsurance from insurers in the normal market.

When considering the documentation work of the captive insurance company, the essential requirement is to provide evidence of cover, both as a legal necessity and to meet contractual and other requirements. In some circumstances the issue of certificates against a master policy will substantially increase the documentation required. Whilst insurance documents are complex and often unwieldy, the captive needs to comply with normal insurance standards to justify the tax deductibility of premiums being paid from one company in the group to another. Even without the legal requirement it is common experience within a large group that the formation of a new in-house insurance company will be treated with scepticism by some executives and they will obviously require proper insurance documentation.

In considering capitalisation in the new captive we are guided by:—

(a) the legal requirements of the country of formation, which may dictate a minimum capitalisation, usually related to the volume of premium retained;

(b) the general credibility of the new company, as too low a capital may suggest a paper operation of insufficient strength, to those who deal with it;

(c) the reinsurers of the new captive will pay great attention to its capital and reserve position. Any shortcoming might cause difficulty in obtaining the necessary reinsurance cover.

Minimum solvency requirements vary from country to country. In Britain, for example, the minimum solvency figure is quite low at 20% for a small company, with the percentage reducing to little more than 10%. The solvency ratio of an insurance company is the ratio between the capital and free reserves on the one hand and the net retained premium on the other. The minimum satisfactory figure is around $33\frac{1}{3}$%, but for a new captive or a very small captive, a figure of 40% or 50% will be more appropriate.

In recent years the solvency margins of many insurers have come under sudden and considerable pressure, usually from two main factors, increases in premiums through inflation and sharp reductions in stock market values. The reduction in stock market values has been as much as 45% or 50% in one year and for the insurance company with a substantial holding of shares the effect on its solvency margin will easily be appreciated. Many insurance companies have also included a substantial property portfolio in their assets and where a drop in stock market values is accompanied by a drop in property values the impact on solvency is even greater.

In times of inflation, property values rise, producing a resulting increase in premium. Taking a rise in premium for inflation in the region of 25% in the course of one year, and with a 40% solvency margin, an increase in capital reserves of 10% would be necessary. For general insurance companies, profitability has not been adequate to finance such increases in capital and reserves from internal sources and we have seen many of the major companies making rights issues to augment their capital base.

The question is often asked as to the minimum amount of premiums at which the captive is viable. The determining factor in establishing a minimum premium is the cost of operation of the captive insurance company compared with the anticipated profits to be derived from assuming a proportion of one's own risk in one's own insurance company. If a premium level of £250,000 will show an anticipated profit of £50,000 and the cost of operation is £25,000, then it might be felt that the resulting profit of £25,000 would show an adequate return. Today, for a captive to be viable, we are almost certainly talking about a premium level in the captive (in net retained terms) of at least £500,000. The relationship between the premium to be retained in the captive and the parent's ordinary annual premium expenditure will vary. If the parent's risks are well spread and non-catastrophic, a large percentage of the premium may be available for retention in the captive, but if its risks are concentrated it may be difficult to find retained premium sufficient to show a profit.

In considering the return on investment from a captive

we are concerned with the investment return from three
sources:—

(a) the capital which is available for investment on a
short or medium term basis according to the likely
cash needs of the captive;

(b) substantial premium funds, which will usually be
available for investment on a relatively short basis,
although as the captive grows and the cash requirements become more predictable, it will be possible
to take more advantage of investment opportunities;

(c) the underwriting profit, which will also provide a
return on investment.

Returning to the accounting needs of the captive, we need
to bear in mind that insurance accounting is quite different
from normal accounting and requires specialist skills. It is
unreasonable to expect an accountant without insurance
experience to make an adequate job of it. Some of the
factors in insurance accounting that need to be borne in
mind are:—

(a) The premium funds of different classes of business
need to be kept separate. The interest earned on
premium funds is usually not included in the funds
themselves, although Lloyd's syndicates follow this
practice.

(b) Each underwriting year is considered a separate
entity and at the end of the financial year, adjustment needs to be made for unearned premiums, un-
paid claims and IBNR (claims that have been incurred
but not yet reported to underwriters).

(c) In terminating an underwriting year, regard must be
paid to the run off of claims that will be incurred over
the following financial years.

(d) Payment of premiums from overseas insurance companies is usually delayed as either the insurance
company or local insurance legislation requires the
maintenance of a reserve or deposit against claims
which have been, or might have been, incurred.

The tax treatment of insurance companies varies substantially between one country and another. It is usual to
separate the underwriting income and the investment income
for tax purposes. In most countries investment income is
taxed on a current year basis but the taxation of underwriting income will always be delayed and throughout the

world, most marine funds are taxed on a three year basis. Insurance company taxation requires specialist skills and there is considerable scope for reducing the tax bill.

One aspect of taxes often forgotten by British companies is that in many countries in the world, premium taxes are payable. The existence of a premium tax provides an incentive for self-insurance without a captive as the tax advantage of paying a premium is reduced. Risks in Australia are in a similar situation with fire brigade charges, because a substantial part of the cost of the fire brigades is met by a percentage levy on insurance premiums. This means that companies self-insuring not only save the expenses of insurers, but avoid contributing to the cost of fire brigades.

The new captive has to decide on a method of underwriting and the three main alternatives available are:—

(a) To use the same basis of rating as that employed by the regular insurance market.

(b) To obtain a reinsurance rate for the captive's business and add to it a sufficient loading to produce a premium that will show a profit to the captive after meeting the cost of reinsurance and cost of losses not covered by reinsurance.

(c) To develop one's own new rating method. This is usually because the parent feels that the method used by the insurance market is inappropriate to its own needs.

The rating techniques used by the regular insurance market can be divided into three main categories. First is **class rating**, where all risks of a certain type, such as an industry, or ship or aircraft, are analysed statistically for claims experience, and a premium is calculated which reflects the claims experience plus a loading for insurers expenses and profit. This technique of rating spreads the losses over the whole of an industry or classification group and has a disadvantage in that it does not reflect, unless special steps are taken, the loss experience of an individual company. The second technique used in the insurance industry, **experience rating,** takes the actual loss experience of the particular client and develops a rate on a cost plus basis. Sometimes this is a pure rate and sometimes the rate is modified by taking out some of the effects of large losses. The third rating technique used by the insurance market when loss experience is not available in an adequate form may be described as **psychological rating,** where the under-writer takes his own view as to the likely loss experience and the rate he will require to insure the risk.

The new captive will need to make arrangements for claim handling. Among the alternatives available are:—

(a) The payment of claims direct by cheque from the captive without any assessment of the claim, depen-dent on either examination of documents or physical inspection by staff.

(b) Use of a loss adjuster who will work on a fee basis.

(c) For liability and similar claims, the use of a lawyer skilled in such claims.

(d) The use of a specialist claims settling agent. Such services are widely available in North America but not generally available in most parts of the world.

(e) To use the claims settling facilities of another insurer or reinsurer.

Reinsurers are very interested in the claims practices of the captives they reinsure and may require the insertion of a reinsurance treaty of either claims control or claims co-operation clauses. In the former case claims will be handled by the reinsurer, and in the latter case the permission of the reinsurer will be necessary before any claims are settled which may affect the reinsurer's results.

In any insurance company, cash flow forecasting can be difficult although, as the scale of operation increases, a greater degree of predictability is usually possible. For liability claims, the usual experience is for small claims to be settled relatively quickly and for large claims to take a number of years, although there is an increasing tendency for payments on account to be made. A similar pattern, but over a much shorter time span, will be found with property claims, with the small claims paid relatively quickly and larger claims paid over some months. Where total loss of a ship or aircraft is involved, the payment of the claim would be very quick. Where a factory is substantially damaged by fire, lengthy loss adjustment will be usual with instalment payments to finance the re-building of the factory.

The cash position of the captive will be similar to that of a normal insurance company but changes may be made to suit the operating needs of either the parent of the cap-tive. For example, premiums may be paid by instalments, but this will have the effect of reducing the investment income available to the captive. Alternatively, claims payments may be delayed until funds are actually required by the operating company and here the investment income of the captive will be increased.

In each case, a cash flow forecast should be made and the range of variability determined. If the forecast is felt to be reliable, short and medium term cash needs can be determined and a suitable investment strategy followed, although one should always allow for a margin of liquidity to meet unexpected needs.

The administrative needs of an insurance company include the provision of an office, staff, communications facilities, especially telex, and, if overseas, the appointment of local directors, who may be needed to satisfy government regulation. This administrative structure is required to meet the following main needs:—

(a) to issue policies and other documents;

(b) to settle claims or instruct others to do so;

(c) to keep accounts as required by the government and by the parent;

(d) to make statutory returns;

(e) to hold board and other meetings as required by law and by the company.

The formation of a captive insurance company provides a major opportunity to obtain, or re-obtain, effective loss control, as operating companies are made to realise that it is their parent's money that is being wasted and not the resources of an insurer outside the group. The most important aspect of good loss control work is to make sure that the motivation of employees is right. Amongst the keys to getting motivaion right are the commitment of top management to loss control on a day-to-day basis, particularly in their comments during visits to operating locations, the use of management accounting systems to record and control losses and what may be crudely called a "stick and carrot" approach. If loss control effectiveness is treated as part of managerial performance then managers will develop and use the necessary skills. If, alternatively, the company says "don't worry—it's insured" then effective loss control is unlikely.

The management method chosen for a captive depends primarily on its type and location. A new captive may be managed by its parent or by outside managers. If managed internally, there may already be an existing organisation that can be developed or a new organisation can be created to meet the situation.

If the experience inside the group is inadequate, the recruitment of experienced specialists is a necessity. Relatively few captives are managed by their own parents, as the cost of managing a new insurance company is prohibitive for all but the largest corporations: anything from £50,000 per annum upwards, with £100,000 as a more likely starting figure. The alternative to in-house management is to appoint an outside company as manager of the captive. Captive management facilities are provided by a number of organisations, including:—

(a) specialist management companies;

(b) underwriting agents and existing insurers, who add managing the captive to the management of other insurance companies;

(c) others, including brokers, lawyers, bankers and accountants who set up specialist companies to manage captives.

There are advantages and disadvantages with each of these methods. Where outside business is to be underwritten, the appointment of an existing underwriting agent is probably the best approach. Where the operation is small and not too complex, it may be possible to use the resources of brokers, lawyers, bankers and accountants but regard has to be had for the dangers of the unskilled manager who may not realise the problems he is making for his client and the difficulty that may be experienced in dealing with other bodies if the captive management is inadequate.

Whilst captive management companies apparently provide the best solution, their skill, experience and expertise varies considerably. The best of such companies are highly competent and their charges reasonable, but there are many captive management companies which are little more than post office operations, so that whilst an economical charge may result, incompetent management may cost much more money than the costs saved.

It may be thought that the formation of a captive will bring independence from the insurance market. It will certainly mean a change of relationship and may provide important buying advantages to the owner of the captive but the insurance market is still necessary and especially the re-insurer. A captive's reinsurance programme is essential to it. Without effective reinsurance a captive cannot continue.

5.17 Reinsurance of Captive Insurance Companies

One of the major advantages that a captive insurance company offers to its owners is the ability to purchase insurance in the reinsurance market. Because this is a wholesale and professional market it operates on much lower expense ratios, so that more of the premium is available for the payment of losses.

A further advantage offered by the reinsurance market is a much wider variety of types of cover. By this, we mean the ability to buy insurance to provide an overall limit of loss on a total of claims basis, or in excess of the stated amount for each claim.

Reinsurance is generally experience-rated so that the premium charge tends to bear a direct relationship to the claims experience of the individual account, unlike direct insurance where the premium charged is often related to the experience of a whole class of similar risks, whose experience may be considerably worse than the individual company concerned.

There are, of course, some compensating disadvantages in the purchase of reinsurance. The low expense ratio tends to mean that fewer services are provided. If the services not provided are large branch network, the economy is a real one, but if detailed loss control services are required, they may not be available from an individual reinsurer. Re-insurance tends to have a high minimum premium and re-insurers are not interested in providing reinsurance services for the really small account. Once this minimum premium level is passed however, there tends to be an economy of scale that is not present in direct insurance.

One of the most important differences in the reinsurance market is the relatively high volatility of premiums. Where losses are experienced in excess of those anticipated, the reinsurer's reaction is usually sharp, with an increase in premium levels quite often accompanied by the increase in the lower level at which the reinsurer will pay claims.

The reinsurance market is a professional buyer's market and those who enter it are assumed to have familiarity with the rules of the game; there is no scope to talk in terms of errors and omissions in placing cover.

5.18 Types of Reinsurance

The oldest type of reinsurance, which is still in consider-able use is **quota share or proportionate reinsurance,** where an insurance company passes to a reinsurer a stated pro-portion of its total business. A 20% quota share would mean that one-fifth of the original risks and one-fifth of the original premium would pass to the reinsurer. As the insurer has incurred considerable expense in obtaining and servic-ing the business, it is customary for the premium passed to the reinsurer to be subject to a deduction in the form of overriding commission. This commission reflects the cost of providing the original services and may range, according to class of business, from $2\frac{1}{2}$% to 30% or more.

Quota share insurance is relatively simple and does, of course, reduce the risks of the 'ceding' insurer to a propor-tion that is acceptable to him. From the point of view of the ceding company, however, it suffers from one major disadvantage. As the size of the risks varies, quite often too much business is being given away.

In order to deal with this disadvantage a new type of re-insurance, **surplus or excess line reinsurance,** came into being. A surplus insurance provides for the ceding insurer to retain a stated amount on each risk thus giving him the maximum desired retention where this is available. Above this stated minimum retention the reinsurer accepts the risk on an excess basis for each risk. With a four line sur-plus treaty, the reinsurance provides protection of up to four times the amount of risk retained by the ceding insurer. Where marine treaties are involved, the term "surplus" is replaced by "excess line" and the amount reinsured is not stated in terms of number of lines, but in terms of an amount of cover, such as £10,000 excess of £2,000 any one voyage.

The biggest disadvantage of surplus treaties is that the premium has to be calculated separately for each risk and where a large portfolio is concerned the amount of clerical work is very considerable. However, surplus treaties do provide a means of keeping as much of the risk as possible and only passing to a reinsurer business that is 'surplus' to one's own retention requirements.

In order to deal with the clerical complexity proposed by surplus insurance, a new form of reinsurance was intro-duced, **'excess loss' reinsurance.** An excess loss treaty pro-vides reinsurance on the basis of the cost of any claim (up to a stated limit) to the extent that it exceeds a stated amount for each loss. For example, an excess loss treaty may provide for £10,000 each and every loss in excess of £5,000 each and every loss. This means that the reinsuring company's losses from a particular incident as defined in the treaty are aggregated and, after the ceding insurers retention has been deducted, the remainder of the claim, up to the limit of the treaty, is payable by the reinsurer.

It is usual to express the reinsurance premium as a percentage of the original net premium. This avoids the need for a great deal of calculation and, unlike surplus reinsurance, it is not necessary for each risk to be notified to the reinsurer. Instead, an approximate premium for the year is calculated in advance and a minimum and deposit premium paid based on this figure. The reinsurance treaty is subject to adjustment when the final premium figures for the year are known. Excess loss treaties may be further divided into two types, "working" and "non-working". For a working excess of loss treaty both parties expect that claims will be incurred and the premium level is fixed accordingly. A non-working treaty provides catastrophe protection and it is expected that in most years no claim will fall under the treaty, but from time to time a particularly poor year for the reinsuring company will result in a potentially heavy claim. If a non-working cover begins to have claims on a regular basis, it will usually be necessary for the retention limits to be lifted to adjust it so that it becomes again a non-working treaty.

The fourth main type of reinsurance is **"stop-loss" or "aggregate loss".** This protection was developed to deal with one of the deficiencies of the excess loss reinsurance treaty. When reinsurance protection is provided on an excess loss basis, the reinsuring underwriter is protected for the excess of a stated amount for each claim or loss. This means that he is protected against the catastrophe loss, but can still be exposed to a large frequency of claims. Protection against this frequency problem can sometimes be achieved by use of a stop-loss treaty. A stop-loss treaty protects the retained account of the reinsuring insurer against an aggregation of claims. Where a total account is protected, the level of protection may be as low as 100% or less of the net premium so that the protection afforded would be to pay up to a stated amount in excess of 100% of original net premium. The addition of the stop-loss reinsurance premium will mean that in such an event the account is certain to make a loss, but the level of loss is contained. For an account that does not expose such a loss level, the effect of the stop-loss reinsurance premium would have been to reduce the net premium, but equally, to limit the size of loss that the account could incur. This type of protection is really appropriate to a new account which may not yet have sufficient spread of risk. As the account develops in size it will soon be found that this protection is not necessary and the reinsurance cost represents an unnecessary burden on the account.

The reinsurance protection of a typical insurance company may well include a combination of all four types of reinsurances. In this way the reinsuring company is able to take advantage of favourable reinsurance facilities either in terms of cover or premium and spread the risk arising from a total account over many reinsurers so as to reduce the loss of all reinsurance facilities from perhaps a single event or series of events.

5.19 Buying Reinsurance

It will be seen that the purchase of reinsurance is a technical matter requiring considerable skill, not only to secure the best terms available but also to make sure that the reinsurance protection selected is completely safe. For most reinsurance it is advisable to use a reinsurance broker, but it is not recommended that the operation be left entirely to a broker. The best results are achieved from close co-operation between the reinsuring company and its broker in terms of selection of market, preparation of data and presentation of claims. When a new reinsurance programme is being prepared, considerable care and effort should be devoted to a skilfully prepared submission which must accurately reflect the real situation whilst presenting the advantages of the reinsuring underwriter's account to the proposed reinsurer. Simplicity and accuracy are the keynote for such submissions.

In selecting a reinsurance broker, attention should be given to the skill of the broker, his experience with similar accounts, the size of his overall account (which will affect his buying power), the degree of control he exercises in monitoring the solvency of markets with whom he places business and his ability to utilise an international market.

Whilst a great deal of work is involved in setting up a

reinsurance programme, once the programme is established it is important to monitor the reinsurance situation regularly and ensure that those involved in the operation and management of the captive fully understand the reinsurance programme and its effects.

5.20   Reinsurance Tactics

It is sometimes felt that the reinsurance programme is simply a matter of buying the best cover available at the cheapest price. However, in view of the volatility and technical character of the reinsurance market, the prudent captive owner will so arrange his reinsurance programme and activity to ensure as far as possible continuity of cover. Good reinsurance results will usually lead to a progressive reduction in the cost of reinsurance protection expressed on a percentage basis.

The first essential in buying reinsurance is to spread the risk so that one is not over-dependent on a particular part of the reinsurance market or a particular reinsurer. Control of loss experience is as important in terms of limiting future reinsurance price as it is in terms of limiting the cost of the captive company of retained losses at present.

The skilled insurance company regards the protection of its reinsurers as the protection of its financial future and from time to time "facultative" (or ad hoc) reinsurance will be purchased to take out of the treaty reinsurance account a potentially hazardous risk. Although this will reduce the profit available to the captive, it will equally reduce the risk of disaster from the impact of a sudden claim which, on reflection, reinsurers might well have expected the ceding insurer to protect them against.

A sophisticated reinsurance plan involving different types of reinsurance in different markets helps to spread the risks and provide long term protection.

As with any other buying and selling operation it is important to understand the thinking, needs and capability of the other party, and reinsurers are no different in this respect. Each reinsurer has a particular type of market that he cultivates and has particular views as to the type of business he seeks, the basis of rating and the extent of protection he is able to give. By bringing the needs of the two parties together, the chance of long term success for both is improved.

In purchasing reinsurance one should always remember

that the claims will be paid in years ahead and the security and stability of the reinsurer is the best protection to make sure that the cover purchased really meets one's needs at the time when one needs to use it.

Involvement for the multi-national parent in its own risk by means of its own captive insurance company is often more easily achieved through reinsurance than a direct basis. In many countries there are substantial restrictions on insurance operations and an insurance company is usually required to become admitted or licensed. A good alternative to licensing is to obtain the services of a friendly large insurer who accepts the risk through his own local office, retains part of the risks for his own account, charges a fee as commission on the reinsurance ceded in return for his services, and passes a proportion of the risk to the captive in the form of reinsurance.

Such fronting arrangements are not always easy to obtain and it is easy to underestimate the amount of work involved for the ceding insurance company. The bigger the volume of premium the easier it will be to find an insurance company that will be interested. The more countries that are involved, the more important it is to use a single insurer or panel of insurers for fronting purposes.

The services provided by such an insurer include the issue of policies and other documentation, accounting in the currency involved, the settlement of claims locally, and sometimes loss control services. It should be noted that very few, even of the largest insurance companies, have a multi-national capability extending to many countries of operation, and it is most important to check the capability of an individual insurer before using him. The fronting fee will certainly be related to the volume and cost of services provided and may often reflect the reluctance of the insurer to provide such a service at all.

A common point of misunderstanding between such companies and their captive reinsurers is the delays that are necessary in moving premiums from many overseas countries, where local regulations require either delay in premium remittance for exchange control reasons, or the withholding of parts of the premium as a local claims reserve. Before embarking on such a captive exercise it is necessary to work out in detail the flow of funds to make sure that sufficient premiums will be available to meet the operating needs of the captive. Where substantial overseas insurance is involved the retentions required under local regulations may starve the captive of funds in its early years.

Some characteristics of reinsurance operations may cause surprise and even dismay for the multi-national becoming involved in reinsurance for the first time. It is customary for reinsurance treaties to contain a provision that reinsurers may inspect the books of the ceding company at any reasonable time. This provision is inserted to protect the reinsurer against subsequent changes in volume or character or risk written by the ceding company.

Reinsuring companies take a great interest in the quality of management and the solvency of a captive, particularly where they are passing large volumes of business to the captive and this is protected by reinsurance.

The reinsurer will therefore expect a captive company to be adequately capitalised and competently managed and will usually require that these two characteristics are demonstrated to its satisfaction. Where doubt still exists about the solvency of a captive, reinsurers sometimes require a guarantee from the parent.

There will usually be stipulations regarding the payment of premium and it should be noted that these must be adhered to. There is not the discretion commonly exercised in direct insurance as to the timing of premium payments. On the other hand, although premium payments will be stipulated, the pattern of instalment paying available in many reinsurance programmes will, in fact, augment the cash flow of the captive in a way that might not otherwise be possible.

From a negative point of view it is quite often necessary to withhold reserves against claims and other premium stipulations, overseas remittances may be delayed by exchange control or other regulations and in most overseas countries premiums are subject to taxes and other payments which may on occasions be borne by the original insurer and therefore deducted from the amount passed to the captive that is reinsuring such an insurer.

5.21 Reinsurance Complexity

It will be seen from even this short description that re-insurance is a somewhat complex business. In addition to the points already made, we would add the following:—

1. Reinsurance treaties are commonly conducted in many currencies where the ceding insurers operations are

widespread. This can result in complex accounting and delayed remittances.

2.   The reserve arrangements for reinsurance treaties are equally complex to the outsider.

3.   Most reinsurance treaties are subject to premium adjustment in the light of the actual out-turn of the ceding company's account, particularly as regards premium volume, although some treaties may be subject to contingent profit commission, depending on the ultimate profitability of the account.

Chapter VI

Risk Management Organisation

6.1 Establishing a Risk Management Programme

The implementation of the risk management programme and the organisational requirements necessary to enable it to be carried through successfully will usually follow on from a detailed study of the company which clarifies its risk profile in relation to both its existing operations and its future corporate objectives. This profile is likely to take the form of a detailed risk identification study, as described in Chapter II of this book, or could be part of a more general overview that examines the company's activities, its assets, earnings and special skills. This overview is also likely to be supplemented by recognition of the overall future objectives and considering these in conjunction with the company's attitude or philosophy to risk and its financial stance on insurance buying.

The company's agreed attitude on risk taking will also play a crucial part in later decisions on policy statements, implementation of the agreed risk management programme and the supporting risk financing philosophy.

Regardless of the format used for the development of the profile, the study will involve discussion with senior management, production of a narrative outlining the investigations and conclusions and the probable development of charts of vulnerability using data available from the sources within the company, and external industry information.

The more detailed identification study is likely to include detailed audits of the company's operations which will comprise identification, measurement and evaluation of loss control and financing. Site visits will also be part of this initial work with study of the company's operations, including evaluation of the risks in the company's suppliers and major customers.

The report which follows the development of the risk profile will be instrumental in persuading management of the necessity for introducing a risk management programme, so presentation is important. Good presentation will emphasise the necessity for the introduction of a considered programme which enables the company to identify major threats to its operations, consider matters of control and provide for the development of a financial strategy to meet losses that occur. Other aspects can include the opportunity for insurance premium savings, reduction in losses and social and political pressures, particularly where these involve compliance with legislation.

The value of risk management as a continuing formal planning technique, which includes a whole range of existing management tools, needs to be emphasised. It should, however, acknowledge that top management are already in the process of managing risk and are usually fully aware of the major threats to their business. It is however likely that in organisations that have not introduced risk management, the system of managing risk is on an informal basis that recognises, in the minds of management, that they understand what might happen and have the capacity to handle such eventualities should they occur.

This "seat-of-the-pants" approach usually means that the management style is likely to be a pragmatic one that decides how to solve the problem after the incident has occurred, rather than on a planned and anticipated basis. This approach has the serious flaw that by the time the risk is considered, it may be too late and that in the rapidly-changing social, political and technological circumstances in which companies now find themselves, the pragmatic approach can be unmanageable and the consequences catastrophic. It needs to be pointed out, in the presentation to top management, that the value of risk management in today's world is the anticipation of the event, preparation for planning should the event occur, including the use of contingency plans and the development of the capacity to handle the problems, rather than simply leaving matters to chance.

The plans for persuading management that risk management should be introduced, will need to be supported by quantification, particularly in terms of reduced cost and reduced probability of large losses. The value of risk management to help companies secure budgeted performances by identifying and controlling threats which reduce operating costs, by reduction of wastage, lost time and insurance premium, needs to be supported by comparison with existing expenditure. Management will expect these benefits to be continually monitored to ensure that they still compare favourably with the cost of the measures originally introduced. Techniques for monitoring can include incident analysis, contingency planning review, safety records, claims experience, premium cost and so on.

Perhaps the most important and contentious aspect of introducing a risk management programme will be answering the question "Who should manage the risks?" Risk management is of course not a panacea for solving all the problems of the company but is a collection of techniques which can be used by line management for managing their own operations and risks. It is important that the advisory nature of the risk manager's job is recognised and the role should be functional in support of top management's commitment to the risk management concept and line management's desire to improve the control of risks within their own activities.

Risk management suffers from the disadvantage of not being a technique which is taught to managers as part of their basic training but if the concept is accepted by a company, they will not only be improving the performance of their company but they will be operating on new ground and in advance of competitors.

6.2 Practical Problems

Possibly the most difficult initial task in introducing the risk management programme will be the organisational question where the risk management function should be located within the company's managerial structure. Because of the historical development of risk management, most existing risk managers have evolved from insurance departments with reporting generally to financial or secretarial executives.

In his book "Risk Management in International Corporations", Norman Baglini*, following reseach within United States corporations, showed quite clearly that this position still dominates and the USA experience almost certainly

---

*Norman Baglini—"Risk Management in International Corporations".

RISK MANAGER—REPORTING RELATIONSHIPS

Report to	Number of Respondents	Per Cent Respondents
1. Treasurer, controller or secretary/ controller	52	32.7
2. Vice-president/ treasurer or vice-president/ controller	33	20.8
3. Vice-president — finance	20	12.6
4. Assistant secretary or assistant treasurer	18	11.3
5. Senior Vice-president, vice-president or general manager	7	4.4
6. Vice-president/ secretary or vice-president — administration	5	3.1
7. President, executive or vice-president or higher	3	1.9
8. Director of personnel or industrial relations	1	0.6
9. Other	18	11.3
No response to	2	1.3
Total of Respondents	159	100.0

CHART 49

applies to other parts of the world. Chart 49 shows the results of his investigations by reporting relationships.

There is, however, no reason why the risk manager cannot be located in a technical department, legal department or any other. The crucial factor is to relate the function of the risk manager as closely as possible to the company's normal style of operation.

6.3 Risk Management in Decentralised Companies

Such problems of location are often exacerbated in companies that have international or multinational operations. The only solution is to try to reflect the managerial and communication systems which are in operation. For example, one should avoid a highly-structured centralised risk management function if the company operates throughout the world on an autonomous divisional basis. In this case the risk manager's role requiring access to management and awareness of the activities of the company in its operational locations would be impossible. In such a decentralised company, it might be more appropriate for risk management representatives to be appointed on a functional basis in each of the locations with the risk management adviser co-ordinating their activities in the same way. This approach is likely to be used in such companies for financial, marketing and other matters.

The role of the risk manager in a company will of course depend to a significant extent on the resources that are available. It will be necessary to evaluate the present resource position of the company by auditing the existing talent, particularly in relation to safety personnel, insurance officers, legal advisers and so on.

The position of the risk management adviser and his own skills will also depend on the structure of the company and in particular its spread of operations. Most risks that arise involve a number of people within the company, all of whom are likely to have different skills, some of whom will have line management responsibilities and others functional responsibilities, similar to that of the risk manager.

The communication ability of the risk manager in such situations is important and his acceptability as a contributor to the manager involved, essential. At the implementation stage, the personality and credibility of the appointed risk manager are probably of paramount importance. This ability, however, will only in the long term be productive if it is supported by a clear commitment from top management and this has traditionally been done at the implementation stage of a risk management programme, by the issue of a policy statement.

6.4 Risk Management Policy Statements

The policy statement will need to explain how risk management is to be implemented within the company, dealing with any changes to the insurance buying philosophy, the appointment of a risk manager or the redefinition of his job and including information on any appointment related to local management's support to the risk management function. (For example, local safety officers, fire wardens.)

An example of a typical policy statement is included in Chart 50.

Policy Statement

1. That the objective of the company is to prevent injury, to all persons with whom the company comes into contact, whether they be employees, customers or members of the community at large.

2. That it is the responsibility of line management to take all steps necessary to avoid losses, injuries or damage to property from any cause or any other factor that could have adverse effects on the company's operations and reputation.

3. That it is the overall objectives of the risk management policy to reduce the company's losses to a minimum, thereby substantially reducing the money spent on insurance premiums and the hidden cost of loss.

CHART 50

Formal written statements of policy are not totally accepted in practice. Baglini's survey of US international companies showed that just under half of the total respondents had no written statement whatsoever. And indeed, there was no relationship between the existence of a written statement and the size of the company. It is important that the commitment of top management in the programme is indicated strongly to line management and that this is supported by a definition of the risk manager's role. This definition should emphasise the advisory relationship that he has with line management and that the responsibility for implementation of the policy lies at operational level where the commitment of the whole workforce is necessary to achieve the desired objectives.

In most implementation programmes, the policy statement initiates the process and needs to be quickly followed by discussions, seminar or manuals which explain the techniques in detail and lay down the details of the implementation programme, including the documentation, reporting systems and so on. Later in this chapter, an outline risk management manual, which could be used for this purpose, is suggested.

Some companies have also introduced, as part of the implementation programme, a top management statement on their own accountability and some of the methods by which the continuing process of monitoring the programme will be carried out.

These statements can include all or some of the following

— encouragement of the board of directors to refer in the company's shareholders' reports and internal presentation, to the company's overall attitude to safety and its aims and success record in this area;

— introduction of a system which supplies to management as a matter of course, detailed explanations of major incidents supported by firm reaction to those incidents that require urgent attention;

— comment by top management during visits to operating units, on the risk and safety situation that they see, including strong comments on examples of poor house-keeping or other adverse physical features noticed by them;

— regular examination of operational trends in incident frequency, supported by explanation and improvement plans where these trends are shown to be adverse;

— inclusion on the agenda of board meetings and executive committee meetings as a fixed item, the safety of the company's operations;

— consideration of the use of safety performance as a criteria in promotional and/or salary reviews;

— inclusion within financial budgets at operational level, the real cost of incidents;

— requirement for the internal audit department of the company to include evaluation of aspects of the risk management process in its checklists.

To summarise the implementation of the programme, the company should aim at four objectives:

1. a written policy communicating the risk management objectives and systems;

2. the necessity for top management to demonstrate that it is to be applied;

3. emphasis on the need for all management to continue to demonstate the application of risk management principles with the long-term aim that general acceptance of risk management should be part of the company's day-by-day operations;

4. emphasis that the whole development process is aimed at producing a mechanism for accountability within the company for controlling the risks that threaten its operation.

6.5 Role of the Risk Manager

Perhaps the first point to make about the risk manager's responsibilities within an organisation is that his job is not that of managing the risks that face the company. In this sense, the title of risk manager can be considered misleading but if we regard the role as a functional one and the risk manager as an adviser or co-ordinator, this probably better describes his activities within the company. In his booklet entitled "The Role of the Risk Manager in Industry and Commerce", J. R. Parkinson said, when discussing the role of the risk manager:

"The man who is called a risk manager is more of a risk management adviser, or, what is possibly better still, a risk management co-ordinator. His job is multidisciplinary and that of a liaison officer. It is necessary for him to develop a liaison with other functions in the company, such as plant managers, work engineers, design engineers, buyers, distribution managers, transport managers, packaging managers, marketing managers, accountants, secretaries and so on and to make it very clear that risk management is the responsibility of all. The job of the risk manager can only be to assist management to identify risks and this is usually possible to do with commonsense laymen's questions.

Having identified the problem, it is necessary to obtain the support and assistance of the other appropriate functions to find an answer to them. In the course of time, an attitude of mind will develop throughout the company, so that all functions are themselves identified risks and thereafter in evaluating and controlling.

It is the risk manager's job to keep up the impetus and to develop the various relationships and to do this, it is necessary for him to travel a great deal. When he visits plants and companies throughout his group, he must involve himself with all aspects of the company's activities and not just ask those questions relevant to what was previously insured. For example, he should know the raw materials involved with the various production processes, where they come from, how many suppliers there are, how many factories the suppliers have, how easy it would be to obtain other suppliers, what is the market situation of the material, how much is used, what the stock situation is, whether the stock is on site and how spread it may be—and these are merely aspects of examining and identifying risks associated with the supply of raw materials. Equally full inquiries have to be made about sales and customer situations. One of the most important aspects of risk management in any factory is, of course, to make sure that the services are fully protected, not only the normal services of gas, water, electricity, oil and light, but also effluent disposal . . .

. . . It is important that the risk manager has an acceptable personality. He must be able to talk at all levels of the company, from top management to shopfloor in such a way that he can be understood. It should not be necessary for him to be dogmatic because, in the main, risk management controls are often matters of opinion which arise out of discussions with the responsibile personnel. He should, nevertheless, be firm and placid for what he considers sensible and necessary measures to protect risk situations. He should have a reasonably high standing in the company, as he would otherwise have difficulty in getting close to senior management and discussing risk management with them."*

When we look at the functions of the risk manager within a company, we can break these down in the following way:

— to help develop risk management within the company;

— to provide an overall view of the company's vulnerabilities and of the management of the risks they entail;

— to train, advise and assist management to manage risk more effectively;

— to provide a specialist knowledge of risk to complement

---

*"Role of the Risk Manager in Commerce and Industry", J. R. Parkinson, published by Keith Shipton Developments Ltd., June 1976.

the specialist expertise provided by others operating within the company;

To help the risk manager fulfil this task will involve the following:

— formulation of a detailed risk management policy within the broad terms of the policy statement agreed by top management;

— evaluation of the cost of this policy;

— advice and assistance to management on the implementation of the risk management policy;

— encouragement to other sections of management to develop risk management systems;

— co-ordination of the systems introduced;

— monitoring of the effectiveness of the systems;

— co-ordination of the efforts of different functions within the company towards achievement of the risk management programme;

— involvement in the company's safety, security and loss-prevention activities;

— advice to management on forward planning in areas in which risk management is likely to be involved, for example, corporate planning, disaster planning and contingency planning.

These overall tasks can be incorporated in the risk manager's job description and a specimen job description is shown in Chart 51.

6.6 Requirements for Risk Manager

We have considered the role of the risk manager, his tasks and a specimen job description. What therefore are the attributes that the risk management adviser or co-ordinator needs to have? We have considered aspects of personality, supported by an agreed position within the company and top management commitment. In addition, the risk manager needs to be curious, showing a strong inclination to follow up clues about his company's business which are likely to involve threats to the company's operations. He or she needs to be imaginative, to be able to envisage the potential of risks, to help to advise new solutions to the problems that these involve. His or her personality needs to

**Specimen Job Description for
a Risk Manager**

1. To provide an advisory service to management at
    all levels in the company on matters connected
    with risk management. In particular this will
    involve:

    (a) advice on the correct identification of risks
        which threaten the company's assets or
        earnings;
    (b) advice on the most appropriate methods of
        evaluation of such risks;
    (c) advice on methods of risk avoidance, reduc-
        tion and control;
    (d) advice on methods of financing residual risks
        after all appropriate measures of reduction
        and control have been taken, including
        advice on insurance and self-insurance, to
        provide the optimum combination of protec-
        tion with economy;
    (e) advice on the investigation of losses and
        where appropriate, obtaining reimbursement
        for them.

2. To record and disseminate information about
    accidents or other losses as circumstances which
    might give rise to accident or loss, in order to
    provide a measure of the effectiveness of existing
    loss-prevention systems and to indicate where
    changes may be necessary.

3. To co-ordinate the efforts of specialists in all
    aspects of risk control and financing throughout
    the company.

4. To initiate and take part in risk management train-
    ing programmes, so as to improve the handling of
    risk within the company.

5. To monitor developments in risk management
    contacts in the risk management field as possible
    theory and practice, to obtain as wide a range of
    and seek to introduce appropriate developments
    into the company.

CHART 51

include the ability to get on with people, to be successful in forming the right relationships. This characteristic will be influential in personal success as much depends in a functional environment on the ability to stay friends with other managers. In addition, he or she should be determined and willing to persist with getting answers to questions that need to be answered in relation to the company's risk situation and to be determined to ensure that problems are solved in the right way and with the right considerations.

The archetype risk manager should also have a balanced attitude to risk, should be a risk taker but should not be reckless, should not be adverse to risk in the sense that seeks safety at all costs. This balanced attitude should be supported by a knowledge of accounting techniques, a deep understanding of the business of his company, including both its commercial and manufacturing practices, a good grasp of insurance and loss control, including fire safety, security and other physical hazards. He or she needs to have an understanding of how people behave and how this behaviour is likely to be translated into risk possibilities.

This description of a risk manager suggests an executive with all-round experience and ability. Few exist and companies have many other uses for such able people. In selecting the risk manager priority should be given to personal qualities with technical knowledge taking second place. Unfortunately insurance managers often do not have the necessary skills and risk managers are now being appointed from line management and other functional positions more closely connected with the mainstream activities of a company.

In general terms, the managerial qualities are the essential requirements for the risk manager operating in a functional capacity, the gaps in technical knowledge can be filled at a later stage, providing the basic requirements are met.

The risk manager at work will be involved closely with both functional colleagues and operating management. Typical risk management tasks would include working with the financial director or treasurer on developing risk-financing strategies, incorporating insurance buying, operational budgets and forms of credit. He or she may work closely with the legal adviser or company secretary on legal liability loss control which are likely to include contractual and statutory liability positions. With the factory manager, he or she may be involved in development of contingency plans, advice on localised loss control measures and project risk management. Similarly these aspects of the risk management world could involve contact with the marketing director and the research director, especially on project risks and product quality and safety control measures.

The risk manager is also likely to be involved in training other members of the company in risk management techniques and this can indeed often be part of normal responsibilities. This training activity could well involve specific training for those involved in the company with accounting, engineering, production and factory or general management tasks. The normal methods of training would be in-house courses, aimed at teaching basic risk management techniques, putting across the emphasis of involvement and motivation at local level and should have the overall objective of securing commitment to the overall risk management programme. Specialist outside courses can also be used, not only for the management of companies, but also for the risk management adviser and these courses are likely to deal with aspects of safety, fire engineering, security problems, insurance, legal liability, particularly products liability and other technical factors involved in the function.

6.7   Risk Management Manual

Once the programme has been established, it is usually the responsibility of the risk management department to disseminate information which can be used by operating management for the carrying out of the agreed programme. Risk management operations manuals are often used. Apart from manuals some companies have used risk management bulletins which explain the company's philosophy and implementation programme. These bulletins are issued on a regular basis with a view to keeping line management up to date with new techniques, to inform them of factors that have developed in other parts of the company, the relevance to their own operations, and also to emphasise the on-going nature of the risk management process. If manuals are used, it is important that these are attractively produced, the message put across graphically and they are kept up to date. Avoidance of risk management jargon is important and if the manuals can be supported by good presentation, involving diagrams, charts and simple case studies, this can all be very helpful.

The index for a typical manual could include the following subjects:

1. Statement of policy, including the company's overall philosophy to the management of risk.

2. What is risk management? This section of the manual needs to emphasise the use of loss-control techniques, the quantifiable results that can be achieved by management in reducing the cost of loss and the necessity for overall support from employers in this endeavour.

3. The range of the overall risk management programme explaining the use of guidelines and formal techniques that will be introduced.

4. A description to the responsibilities of line management in applying risk management to their day-to-day activities.

5. A detailed exposition of the real cost of loss with examples and its effect on the company's profit and reputation.

6. A checklist of risk classifications explaining in detail the areas that line management should be constantly searching for, also supported by real examples.

7. Mock-ups of risk exposure charts, usually within the company, with an explanation of how they are to be completed and used by both line management and the risk manager.

8. An explanation of the acceptable techniques used by the company for controlling loss.

9. An outline of the role of risk management, in both induction and on-the-job training programmes and how this fits into the overall risk management process.

10. Details of the systems to be used for recording losses including calculation of their total cost to the company.

11. Copies of specimen forms to be used by management for recording of incidents, analysis of incidents, detailing trend and the causes and effects of loss prevention, both positive and negative.

12. Specimens of forms to be used for the evaluation of controls including loss reduction or analysis and methods of quantifying savings.

13. A detailed explanation of the self-insurance philosophy
     of the company and its current and potential benefits
     in real terms, possibly as a relation to the turnover or
     earnings of the company or the local operating unit
     involved. In the overall implementation process,
     account needs to be taken of the psychological pro-
     blems involved with the introduction of risk manage-
     ment and particularly avoidance of it being seen as
     an overlap with the responsibilities of the line manager.
     It is important that the overall approach is to identify
     with the line manager's own estimation of his job and
     to avoid any suggestion that the work of the risk
     management adviser is a threat to his expertise or his
     task in carrying out his day-to-day activities.

It is important that the job of risk management is seen
within the company as part of the duties of each manager
and each specialist. Any possibility of risk management
being seen as something imposed from outside is likely to
result in resistance to the process. It is in addition essential
for the success of the programme that the person in the
operating position is actively involved in the management
of the risk within his own area of responsibility and sees
the central risk management advisory function as an aid to
his own work and part of the overall integrated risk management philosophy of his company's operations.

Chapter VII

The Management of Non-Insurable Risk

7.1 Types of Non-insurable Risk

Chart 52 shows, in somewhat arbitrary fashion, seven different approaches to the management of non-insurable risk, (although individual aspects under several of the headings can be insured). Let us consider each in turn.

Project risk management has evolved to deal with the problem illustrated by the increasing number of projects which fail to be completed on time and within budget. It

PROJECT	— Identify threats to on-time and on-budget performance.
COMPUTER	— Vulnerabilities arising from use of electronic data processing.
POLITICAL	— Recognising threats in all of the company's environment, keeping company in balance with environment, managing relationship.
COMMERCIAL	— Evaluating risk trade-off to realise (as far as possible) the company's potential.
SOCIAL	— Recognising system imbalance in society (wrong trade-off decisions). Helping develop more effective solutions.
PERSONAL	— Handling physical threats, incl. wastage relationships, coping with change.
MILITARY	— All military expenditure and activity is a risk trade-off decision.

CHART 52—NON-INSURABLE ASPECTS OF
RISK MANAGEMENT

uses as its starting point the techniques of critical path analysis, but focuses sharply on the major potential threats to the completion of major projects on time and within budget.

Taken from a paper on the subject of project risk management*, Chart 53 gives an illustration of the range of project uncertainties.

COMPLETION
● Problems with Suppliers
● Problems with Contractors
● Unexpected Commissioning Problems
● Dislocations of Transport
● Errors in Planning
● Damage to Construction Resources

PRODUCTION
● Fortuitous Damage
● Malicious Acts and Sabotage
● Political Risks
● Dislocations in Supplies/ Services
● Customer Disabilities
● Dislocations in Labour
● Consumerism
● Impairment of Credit

?
EXPECTED FLOW
OF EARNINGS

PERFORMANCE
● Errors in Research
● Failure of New Technology
● 'Bugs'
● Faulty Equipment
● Labour Unavailable, Cannot Master Skills, Dislikes Job

DEMAND
● Changes in Economy
● Absence of Forecast Demand
● Changes in Social Habits
● Changes in Competition
● Hazardous Product

COST
● Errors in Forecasts
● Changes in Price
● Action of Financiers
● Changes in Economy
● Actions of Monopolies
● Changes in Wages
● Damage
● Liability
● Ransom
● Waste

CHART 53—THE RANGE OF PROJECT UNCERTAINTIES

---

* "Project Risk Management", 'Foresight—the Journal of Risk Management' Vol. 1 No. 5, November, 1975.

Computer risk management applies a similar approach to recognising and handling the major threats to an electronic data processing system. The very character of an EDP system means that the company or organisation owning the EDP installation will tend to become more vulnerable as it makes greater use of the EDP system, unless steps are taken to recognise the new vulnerabilities.

Indeed, the more effective the computer system in reducing unnecessary duplication of work and the more successful it is in handling problems for its parent organisation, the more the risk of the parent organisation will be concentrated at that particular point. This is a further illustration of the concept of trade-off. We enjoy the advantages of the computer but we need to recognise the disadvantage of increased dependence and vulnerability. Computer risk management therefore deals with physical threats in the insurable risk area, with dependencies on staff (especially in relation to the high turnover of computer staff), software and the attraction of the computer to certain types of vandals and saboteurs. The main elements of computer risk management are shown in Chart 54.

Political risk management takes a much broader view and deals with the identification and management of all the major threats in the company's environment. Some of these threats have obvious political connotations, such as legislation, aimed at particular organisations, which imposes penalties or prevents such companies from fulfilling their objectives. The techniques of political risk management underline the fact that all legislation and political activity is originally founded on opinions and view which a significant section (although not usually a majority) of the population hold. The views can partially be the result of political agitation, but agitation will not normally be successful without a feeling of grievance for it to work upon. The feeling of grievance may be due to real defects in the political structure or system or may be due to failures of communication which permits sectors of the population to feel they have been unreasonably treated. The positive techniques of political risk management are therefore concerned with identifying changes in the company's environment that could threaten it, understanding those changes and making sure the company responds to them. In some cases, political risk management will mean changing the company's objectives because the original objectives are

1. Use property/earning risk control sheets (fire/explosion/theft)
    Charts 37, 38, 39

2. Differences between manual/machine/computer operations:
    a) invisibility of computer data/processing
    b) concentration—dependence and criminal opportunity
    c) loss of manual skill and control

3. Technology
    a) operations   — data input
                           — data output including printing/display
                           — sorting
                           — calculating
    b) inputs   — paper tape
                           — punched cards
                           — magnetic tapes
    c) storage media   — magnetic tapes   cheap/slow
                           — magnetic disc   dearer/faster
                           — core storage   dearer/faster
    d) remember access requirements
    e) processing modes   — batch
                           — real time
    f) function   — operating
                           — system analysis
                           — programming
                           — data input
    g) distributed processing — can reduce some vulnerabilities

4. Exposures
    a) equipment
    b) data
    c) capability to perform (from inside or outside events)
    d) loss of know-how
    e) fraudulent manipulation
    watch service dependability in light of concentration and required
    time response
    e.g. wage systems
        air-traffic — other safety process control
        customer service — airline check-in
        real time — telephone and other links
    remember enhanced possibilities of arson/malicious damage

5. Control techniques
    a) separation of responsibilities
    b) back-up machines, programmes, records
    c) accountability — insistence on plain language
    d) control unnecessary publicity
    e) make sure trade-off economy against vulnerability is understood
       by management
    f) before we begin any computer project — check our resources
       and capability (and those of suppliers as well as experience)
       before commitment to abandon previous system or make major
       new investment

    (Can we fall off the cliff? i.e. no way back)

CHART 54—COMPUTER RISK CONTROL

no longer possible in the new environment in which the company operates. In other cases, the technique will be more in the nature of the company presenting its own story more effectively to its neighbours and employees.

Commercial risk management has been discussed earlier and it is included for the sake of completeness. It will be seen, however, that the common elements of identification, measurement and control of the risk are very similar in each of the techniques.

Social risk management has not so far been examined. Social risk is the impact on individual, organisation and community of changes in man's thinking, habits and attitudes. Its subject matter is the continuing change in social attitudes and activity. A typical social risk management problem would be the bankruptcy of a large city due to the parallel trends of large companies moving out of the city (thus eroding its tax base) whilst considerable local expenditure is needed to deal with new social problems that arise from the breakdown of the city's fabric. Other social risk management problems are vandalism, football violence, over crowding of leisure activities, derelict urban areas, and the changing use of the countryside. The progressive degradation of public transport as private motoring expands can be expected to be another social risk management problem.

The techniques of social risk management are therefore concerned with identifying the changes taking place in the world around us and locating the causes of those changes, so that the problem can be better understood and effective action taken at personal, company and community level. Most social risk management problems also reflect violence in trade-offs. Imbalances arise when, because of limitations in the social or political system, the benefits of a certain change are enjoyed by one group of individuals or companies, whilst the disadvantages are suffered by another. Where such imbalance is marked, other groups of individuals and companies will identify it as an opportunity, and the trend will be accelerated, with a parallel rising sense of grievance on the part of those who suffer the disadvantages without enjoying any of the benefits. A typical example would be a new, lively and therefore noisy, social club or converted inn, which is successful, and attracts large numbers of motoring customers from a wide area, causing congestion and annoyance to local inhabitants, who do not wish to enjoy its facilities. These local houseowners will suffer a diminution in the value of their property, but have no means of recovering that reduction in value from those who have benefited from the change.

It should not be implied that the financial advantages to one party are exactly balanced by the financial disadvantages to the other parties. This may be the case, or there may be an overall profound imbalance so that there is a considerable net advantage or net disadvantage to the whole area.

Personal risk management stems from the fact that we live in a world with new threats, a world that is changing much more rapidly than ever before, and a world with much greater systems vulnerabilitiies and dependencies so that there is a developing need for personal homeiostesis. A good illustration of the physical aspects of personal risk management was the London Weekend Television's series "Stay Alive", following which Eric Clark wrote a paperback advertised as "Essential know-how for dealing with hundreds of threats to our lives—in the jungle, sea, the air, and desert, in snow and ice . . . and not forgetting those two accident blackspots the home and the roads. All the do's and don'ts are there, self-defence included and some very practical advice on staying out of danger."

A wide range of literature has sprung up giving advice on how to cope with a wide variety of new threats, including how to get a job or how to keep a job. Such books are not new; they have been a feature of the commercial scene for the last 100 or so years, with titles such as "How to Succeed in Business". What is interesting is the changing emphasis from seeking competitive success to finding means of survival. A broad approach to personal risk management could include not only handling physical threats, but also handling the more difficult social relationships of today's world and coping with a change in general.

Military risk management is the concern of defence planners and deserves only a brief mention here. The whole concept of armed forces is a response to a threat, so that defence expenditure must of necessity be a risk management expenditure. All military expenditure and each military decision must be a trade-off decision. Indeed, the current dilemma of many governments in deciding defence priorities reflects an essential part of our earlier definition of risk management, the concept of "economic control".

It is impossible to devise a military system today that provides complete defence against all military threats, and because of cost one has to limit defence expenditure to that which is considered economically justified to deal with the main threats.

The very concept of deterrent military expenditure reflects both system vulnerability and the need to balance the system.

This short excursion into some of the wider applications of risk management has been intended to present a broad view to the reader, as the wider the view taken, the more one can successfully prepare plans to deal with threats and take advantage of risk opportunities. Most of this book, has, of course, dealt primarily with risk management techniques in the insurable risk area, but in most cases a little thought will show that those techniques can be applied across the whole range of activities in Chart 52 and to many other areas not specifically mentioned there.

Chapter VIII

Constituent Disciplines of Risk Management

8.1 Disciplines in Current Use

Earlier in this book we have considered how, until quite recently, commercial risk has been treated quite separately from insurable risk and noted that most of the text books on management have limited their scope to insurable risk. This has meant that risk management has tended to draw on insurance for its basic techniques, with a slow development from treating insurance as the main element in the study, to emphasis on risk, with its financing (or insurance) as a secondary factor.

The teaching of risk management has tended to be concerned with insurable risk and has followed the pattern amongst insurance education in being essentially limited to a description of method without relating the work that is performed in the particular area to a wider view of either the company or the economy.

Whilst consideration of risk and how to handle it forms part of many disciplines and is inevitably a part of the work of each manager, there is no all-embracing approach to risk management and indeed many people who manage risk do not use the phrase "risk management" at all.

As a result there is an almost limitless amount of information on the analysis, measurement and handling of risk either by control or by financing but this information is not collated. This is a most curious situation because the management of future uncertainty is undoubtedly one of the biggest problems facing every manager and every enterprise.

In Chart 55 we put forward a necessarily somewhat arbitrary view of main sources of risk management "technology". Here we have grouped sources of risk management thinking under the three headings of under-standing risk, controlling loss (risk) and risk management as an organisational activity.

1. **RISK AS A FACTOR IN EVERYDAY LIFE**

2. **UNDERSTANDING RISK** requires a theoretical base
   - (i) PROBABILITY
   - (ii) ECONOMICS
   - (iii) OPERATIONAL RESEARCH
   - (iv) SYSTEMS THEORY
   - (v) DECISION THEORY
   - (vi) PSYCHOLOGY AND BEHAVIOURAL SCIENCE

   Note: Five different areas of development:—
   Not yet integrated or mutually recognised

3. **CONTROLLING LOSS**
   Unlike 'Understanding Risk' this starts (and usually ends) with practice.
   - (i) Insurance
   - (ii) Loss Control
   - (iii) Self-Insurance
   - (iv) Man as Risk Factor

4. **RISK MANAGEMENT**
   Little specialisation in management generally until 20th century

F. W. Taylor	— Division of management Planning
Henri Fayol	— Security as a separate management function
Safety Officers	— To comply with legislation To reduce cost
Insurance Managers	— Specialist knowledge Usually recruited from insurance industry "Academic Impact"— U.E. Study of insurance in universities Risk analysis on prelude to insurance Concept of Corporate Risk Management
Now being recognised	— Risk is too important to leave to "risk managers" Danger of functionalism Need for organisation framework to manage risk

CHART 55—SOURCES OF RISK MANAGEMENT

In a related area the extensive use of statistics has permitted the development of hazard and reliability analysis. Large tables have been built up to show the reliability under normal operating circumstances of individual items of equipment.

A practical problem that is experienced in all applications of statistics to risk decisions relating to the future is that statistics are based on a past situation that usually does not exist in the same form. In some cases the situation is changing slowly and almost imperceptibly and the figures

To understand risk requires a theoretical base, and we have selected five contributing disciplines: probability theory, economics, operational research, systems theory and decision theory.

8.2 The origins of Probability Theory

Probability Theory can be traced to Galileo's work "Sulle Scopere Dei Dadi" discussing the probabilities of a particular number of combination of numbers in the use of dice. Subsequent work broadened the mathematical base and in the eighteenth century Jacob Bernoulli put forward in "Ars Conjectandi" the first statement of probability theory. From this early theoretical work has sprung the development of both actuarial science and the theory of risk.

The development of a statistical base for such work has of course been dependent on the availability of suitable methods of collecting and sorting statistics. Punched card machines have given way to computers and in relation to mortality of humans, actuarial science is very well developed.

From this first, reasonably reliable base in mortality tables, actuaries have sought to expand their techniques for use in the non-life field. In this task they have so far been thwarted by the lack of adequate statistical information and the much wider variability than so far experienced in connection with human mortality.

The Scandinavian practitioners of "risk theory" have developed a mathematical base for analysing long term insurance funds and their operations. For funds whose limit of loss is cut off at a relatively low level by reinsurance, there is no doubt that such mathematical work has been of assistance in detecting trends and helping to improve the effective operation of the fund, but at this point the application of risk theory to high level reinsurance is still largely theoretical.

will therefore be of considerable value, but in other cases the situation is changing quite dramatically and past figures may be almost meaningless in relation to future decision making. In most situations, however, application of measurement based on probability helps us to understand the problem, even if it does not supply the answer.

8.3 Economics

The second discipline to contribute to an understanding of risk is economics. Because of its very wide base and application covering economic systems, the discipline of economics tends to focus on both a large scale view and implicit or modern economics in acceptance of the need for understanding change. Indeed the biggest problem facing economists in the 20th century has been that of applying economic theories based on analysis of the past to a future situation that would not reflect the same circumstances as that which have produced the past situation. Sometimes the gap between theory and practice has been due to inadequate theory and in other cases it has been due to failure to anticipate the impact of man's activities in changing the economic environment.

Economists approach risk management with one great advantage over many other disciplines: Economics includes an understanding of both systems and change.

It is generally recognised that modern economics began with Adam Smith's work "The Wealth of Nations", published in 1776, and putting forward a broad theory of commercial activity. Within this broad framework Adam Smith looked specifically at risk and suggested a relationship between the uncertainty of an enterprise and the rate of reward:

"In all the different employments of stock, the ordinary rate of profit varies more or less with the certainty or uncertainty of the returns. These are in general less uncertain inland than in the foreign trade, and in some branches of foreign trade than in others; in the trade to North America, for example, than in that to Jamaica. The ordinary rate of profit always rises more or less with the risk. It does not, however, seem to rise in proportion to it, or so as to compensate it completely."

He even gives advice on the subject of self-insurance:

"Sea risk is more alarming to the greater part of people, and the proportion of ships insured to those not insured is much greater. Many sail, however, at all seasons and even in time of war, without any insurance. This may sometimes perhaps be done without any improvements. When a great company, or even a great merchant, has 20 or 30 ships at sea, they may, as it were, insure one another. The premium saved upon them all, may more than compensate such losses as they are likely to meet with in the common course of chances."

Over one hundred years later, Alfred Marshall in "The Principles of Economics"* showed how demand for a particular product is related to a consumer's concept of its value or "utility" to him. Utility in this sense is in terms of the satisfaction, pleasure, or need—fulfilment that the consumer derives from use of some quantity of goods or services. From this basic statement is derived the marketing idea of a difference between price and value. The value to an individual consumer will depend on how he sees his own need of that product or service, and collectively the overall view helps to determine the price. From the point of view of the buyer he is therefore concerned with his own cost of production and the price at which he can sell. He has control over the first factor but much less control over the second. His risk lies in this difference of control.

The whole basis for trade-off lies in the ability of one partner in the transaction to reduce uncertainty for another. It must be based on the differential personal values assumed in different "utilities" or different views of what a particular product or situation is worth or means.

The key economic work in relation to the development of understanding risk is that of Frank Knight, "Risk, Uncertainty and Profit", with which we opened this book. In this most important work Frank Knight puts forwards the first broad conceptual analysis of risk and methods of managing risk. Whilst distinguishing between insurable and non-insurable situations it is apparent that he does not accept the arbitrary distinction between so called "static" or insurable risk and "dynamic" (and presumably non-insurable) risk.

In particular, he deals with two widely used insurance techniques for managing risk, that of classification and consolidation, and shows that both are regularly applied to deal with commercial risk. By classification we mean the collection of statistics under headings which are thought to distinguish appropriately between different risks so as to produce a rough estimate of the future cost of risk applied

---

* "The Principles of Economics", Alfred Marshall.

to a class and in this way so reduce uncertainty. By consolidation we refer to the technique of grouping many risks so as to produce an overall favourable outcome, even though the results of one particular risk may be unfavourable. As an illustration "the law of large numbers" applies to both insurable and non-insurable situations, the only distinction being that when it is applied to an insurable situation it is called insurance.

Frank Knight also provides an interesting link with probability theory and specifically examines the limitations in the analysis of risk and as a guide to taking decisions about the future.

8.4 Operational Research

The remaining three categories under the heading of "Understanding Risk" in Chart 55 are not yet fully linked to each other or to probability theory and economics. Operational research or "operations research" as it is still known in North America, originated with the application of mathematics and multi-disciplinary techniques to the solution of military problems in the Second World War. Most writers on operational research have found difficulty in defining it explicitly. A useful definition is in "Some Techniques of Operational Research" edited by B. T. Houlden and published in 1962.

"In some ways operational research is a method of approach to problems: looking at the whole system first and considering whether altering the factors directly involved in the problem posed will affect other parts of the system . . . Once these interactions have been understood, the operational research scientist can then look into the finer details of the problem if this is necessary.

Operational research also has the characteristic that it is done by teams of scientists drawn from the various graduate disciplines such as mathematics, statistics, economics, engineering, physics, etc."*

It is not suggested that operational research was designed as a technique to deal with uncertainty. In fact most operational research problems are known at least in outline and the brief for an O.R. study usually starts with a problem definition accompanied by a target in terms of possible improvements of productivity, output, or cost.

---

* B. T. Houlden, ed. "Some Techniques of Operational Research".

Operational research often deals, however, with uncertainty, and the handling of uncertainty was immediately the major problem facing O.R. teams and O.R. scientists. The important aspects of operational research from the point of view of the development of risk management were, first, the use of multi-disciplinary techniques, enabling a problem to be examined from different viewpoints, secondly, the implicit understanding that the problem was part of a system or systems, and, thirdly, the development of a "model", usually expressed as a series of mathematical equations to state the variables in the problem and their assumed inter-relationships. Operational research scientists have achieved very substantial economies in the work of large companies and systems but often operational research has not met its expected target because of the normal gulf between day-by-day management and the specialist or the specialists looking at an operational problem from outside.

8.5 Systems Theory

Although there is a great deal of systems thinking in the work of 19th century philosophers, particularly the German materialists, the systems approach has been developed and put forward explicitly within the last 30 years. The essential elements of systems theory is to present a view of the world, or particular parts of the world, as consisting of continually changing systems inter-related to each other. The background to systems thinking has been put by John Beishon and Geoff Peters of the Open University as follows:

"In the slow development of knowledge about the physical and biological world, the most significant advances generally come from painstaking, detailed study and analysis of other smaller areas of knowledge and application. The natural philosophy of the earlier scientists gradually developed into the major natural sciences, physics, chemistry and biology; these in turn have been increasingly sub-divided into subjects such as nuclear physics, polymer chemistry, molecular biology and so on. By the middle of the 20th century this sub-division process had chopped reality and the phenomenon of the real world into hundreds of individual subjects and areas of professional expertise. Knowledge was compartmentalised and departmentalised into small and seemingly more manageable chunks.

The success of analytical techniques, and in particular structural analysis, tended to concentrate attention even on static and structural properties, and some writers have seen this as a reflection of the desire of men to live in well-ordered, static social and political environments. Victorian man might fit into this picture but not the more modern variety. At least two groups found this approach limiting and helpful: the mechanical and later the electrical engineer who wanted to build and run mechanisms and devices which worked and the psychologist or ethnologist who was interested less in the anatomy of the human or animal system than in the behaviour of the complete organism . . .

The impetus towards systems thinking and the systems approach has come from a recognition (some would say a belated recognition) of the complex behaviour which can and does arise from both natural and man-made systems. The long-term implications of systems behaviour gradually become apparent. It is often only when these are seen to threaten human life or living styles that attention is directed to the systems' activity, often in a dramatic way. Another stimulus to adopt a systems approach arises from our attempts to predict and control the behaviour of systems instead of passively suffering from, or just reacting to, the often mysterious changes which occur in the surrounding physical, logical, social, economic and political climate. Attempts to exercise control over systems, whether human or economic, have not been notably successful and, for example, there are real fears being expressed that control is no longer even possible over some of the ecosystems we have constructed or interfered with." *

It is the recognition that the situations in which we are trying to predict and manage uncertainty contain the complexity of many different systems, inter-reacting with each other at different levels, that sets the framework for a new approach to the management of risk and makes the practical handling of uncertainty possible. In order to understand the potential variability of our stated situation in the future, we need to analyse the main factors at work in that situation, to establish how they are changing and to deduce from our study how they are likely to change in the future.

---

* J. Beishon and G. Peters, "Systems Behaviour".

8.6 Psychology and Behavioural Science

Risk management is essentially concerned with events that could disrupt the pattern of future activity or expectations for individual, company or government. Some of these loss-causing events are beyond man's control at least as far as inception of risk is concerned such as lightning, flood, earthquake (although in each case we can use risk management to limit the effects of these risks by control measures).

Most loss-causing events are directly or indirectly related to human behaviour. Many losses are attributed to so called "human error"; other losses would not have happened without human intervention. We can sub-divide losses resulting from human action into three categories:—

1. Deliberate—actions intended to harm. The results of such deliberate harmful action might well be different from those expected by penetrators or victims. Examples are arson, hijacking, kidnap, terrorism and vandalism.

2. Inadvertent—losses resulting from lack of care or any situation where the result is (negatively) different from that intended. Examples include poor design, poor manufacture, poor planning, poor control or inadequate response to external hazards.

3. Completely accidental (i.e. after intervention that is neither deliberate or inadvertent) such as losses resulting from lack of technical knowledge such as the two crashes of Comet airlines due to pressure failure of the fuselage (in turn due to lack of knowledge with the then current "state of the art").

Most losses involve some element of human error and it is helpful to consider the behavioural and/or psychological elements. By considering how human beings will behave in different circumstances we can take account of that behaviour in designing systems and methods of loss control. A good example of application of this approach would be the removal of or redesign of switches that, although correctly labelled, could confuse. We can include in our planning a review of how equipment can be deliberately or inadvertently misused—where such misuse has potentially dangerous consequences we can redesign equipment or systems.

By linking analysis of critical items of equipment or critical segments of operating procedures with a knowledge of human behaviour we can design out a great deal of human error.

8.7   Decision Theory

Decision theory originated as an operational research technique, but is today usually considered as a completely separate discipline. Decision theory uses the elements of probability theory and attempts to apply them to the commercial decisions faced by a manager in his day-to-day and longer term work. Its main field of application is by calculating values for the outcome of different alternative decisions or combinations of decision. From a simple single choice situation the concept has been developed to deal with future multi-choice situations by the use of decision trees, so that today's decision is examined in the light of further decisions that will have to be taken in the future if a particular path is selected today. This enables one to rationalise or optimise the decision made today to take account of potentially negative or positive situations in the future.

The use of decision theory and decision trees in business is still relatively limited, but it has been given considerable impetus in recent years by the work at the Harvard Business School. Certainly decision theory and decision trees are used by a number of large organisations and banks, but there is no evidence that they use them as other than a supplementary guide to decision making.

There is a very human problem in the application of decision theory and decision trees to risk-taking decisions, in that the typical individual in a typical organisation has a great deal to fear from the very low probability disaster compared with his very tiny personal gain from optimising this particular decision. This is also a danger for the organisation, as a simple example may illustrate. To assume that the probability of a certain event is, say, one in a hundred thousand with a cost, if it occurs, of £10 million, may enable one to conclude that the cost of risk is £100 but in practice that is a theoretical abstraction. The most likely result is that nothing will happen but there is also the possibility that disaster will result. In essence, decision trees add a series of such "results" to provide a basis for comparison. When used by someone who understands the consequences of what he is doing, they are a most valuable tool but without this qualification they can be highly dangerous.

An extension of decision theory is its application to decisions made under competitive circumstances where the future outcome to the decision taker is partially or largely determined by the possible alternative actions of a competitor. From a risk management point of view in such a situation we have to take into account, in our risk management decisions, the likely and possible risk management decisions of our competitor as his success or otherwise will directly affect our future financial prospects. Game theory, first developed by von Neumann and Morgenstern*, is useful for assessing the possible alternatives open to a competitor but it does require a good knowledge of the competitor's philosophy and psychology to assess the probability of his selecting a particular course of action. To conclude our consideration of disciplines that are useful in understanding risk, it is important to emphasise that the contribution of each discipline is very different in degree at the present moment and some of the disciplines have more promise for the future than practical use at the moment. However the combined use of all five of these disciplines in an effective way in a risk situation would produce a much better understanding than is usually available to the business man or "risk manager".

8.8   Techniques for Controlling Risk

The second part of Chart 55 deals with practical techniques for controlling loss or risk. Man has always been involved in activities to control risk. Sometimes these have taken the form of practical measures, such as the placing of a home at the top of a tree to avoid wild animals, the location of villages above the flood plain, and the use of walls as a means of defence. Some risk management techniques have been financial and organisational, such as the grouping of individuals for collective defence or the reduced risk that has normally been found by multiplying the number of units involved in a particular type of activity.

Insurance is a most important technique for reducing the financial impact of uncertainty and marine insurance certainly dates back hundreds of years. The evolution of insurance techniques has been relatively slow with occasional dramatic steps forward such as the introduction of many new types of insurance in the early part of this century and the rapid development of insurance techniques in the last twenty five years.

---

* "Theory of Games and Economic Behaviour", J. von Neumann and O. Morgenstern, New York, J. Wiley and Sons, 1964.

There has been a parallel activity in organised loss control with the development of police forces, fire brigades and fire and crime technology.

It is interesting to note that insurance and loss control have often been seen as alternatives and are rarely applied in complete unison. Most insurers offer loss control services, but many of those services are seen by many policy holders as a necessary condition of obtaining insurance rather than an improvement in their overall capacity to control loss.

Recent years have seen the development of self-insurance as a technique, partly to cover uninsurable risks and partly to reduce insurance cost. It has often been argued that self-insurance is a misnomer for non-insurance, but it is beginning to be recognised that a conscious decision not to insure when there is sufficient spread of risk within a company or group can, in fact, be logically regarded as self-insurance. In most countries self-insurance is impeded by the inability to fund for future losses without tax penalty, which gives a competitive advantage to the insurer. The development of captive insurance companies is partly a recognition of the tax advantages of insurers compared with non-insurers (and even more so when such companies are formed off shore) and partly a logical development in scale of self-insurance.

When a commercial company enters the insurance market by participation, through its own insurance company, in its own risk, the whole risk strategy of the firm tends to change. For the first time in the history of the company, there is a conscious evaluation of risk according to financing alternatives.

Perhaps the most important factor in control of loss or risk is man. Looking back through history this is self-evident but the rapid industrial development of the last one hundred years, accompanied by more and more specialisation, has often meant a tendency, inadvertent or deliberate, to replace man as the main factor in loss or risk control.

Over-reliance on mechanical, electronic and other automatic systems has not prevented increasing fire wastage and other losses. There is today an increasing focus on what is called "human error" and a number of techniques are being used to remove the imbalance between man and machine. Ergonomics, which has been defined as "the scientific study of the relationship between man and his working environment" uses techniques from anatomy, human physiology and applied psychology in an attempt to improve man's performance at work, and to deal with some of the disadvantages incurred in practice. At an every day level ergonomics may reduce fatigue and produce more comfortable working conditions; at the extraordinary level an ergonomics approach may be the key to avoiding a future disaster resulting either from fatigue or confusion or even sheer boredom on the part of the operator. The third element in Chart 55 is the state of risk management as a job. Until the beginning of this century (and much later in many individual organisations) there was no specialisation in management. The manager was responsible for all of the functions of management and the only assistance available to him was direction from the proprietor or proprietors and clerical assistance from below. Around the turn of the century the use of "scientific management" began, first with F. W. Taylor's principles of specialisation amongst operations, followed by Henri Fayol's division of business operations into six groups with implicitly separate functional specialist for each. It is interesting that Fayol's six groups, technical, commercial, financial, security, accounting and administrative included, almost automatically, a risk function in the shape of security.

The development of specialist functional managers has subsequently led to several parallel functions in the field of risk such as safety officers, fire officers, security officers, insurance managers and now risk managers. The confusion which this multiplicity in (often necessary) separate jobs has created is shown by the fact that safety officers are sometimes still seen as part of the personnel function. Fortunately, more often, they are now regarded as part of the risk management process.

Fire and security officers arose from management's need to take care of what Fayol called the security function, but safety officers often appeared for a quite different reason, to comply with legislation designed to safeguard employees.

It is perhaps inevitable that industry has to grow to a certain size in terms of units before it becomes economic to employ a specialist insurance manager, and even today the majority or insurance managers are recruited from the insurance industry. The lack of integration of risk management is shown by the fact that the activities of the insurance managers are often kept quite separate from those specialists in the field of fire, security and safety to say nothing of commercial risk.

The accelerating trend towards risk management and the resulting theoretical confusion when insurance managers became risk managers, has brought a focus on risk in commerce and industry that is underlined by other practical necessities. Increasing concentration of risk into single units, increasing size of exposure at those units and changing social habits make the management of risk an urgent task for every business and enterprise today.

Appendices

Checklist 1—Risk Financing and Insurance

Role of Insurance Department
- exposures arising
- controls/systems etc.

Location of insurance buying decisions
- control fully within structure
- advisory capacity
- operators can buy independently without reference or contrary to advice

Insurance buying approach
- direct and intermediaries
- broad extent of direct buying
- intermediaries, their roles, structure and location
- is latter right for the needs of the Group?
- commission discounted by direct insurers and intermediaries

Financial Information about:
- insurances bought direct or through intermediaries
- total premiums and split between direct and each intermediary
- premium totals for each insurer used (discuss these broadly)

Intermediary service
- loss statistics and in what form
- uninsured loss recoveries (recovery role on motor losses and 'loss of use')
- insurance buying
- insurance advice
- claims handling
- claims settlement monitoring with position reports
- self-insurance advice
- administrative work direct with operating units (relationships)

— joint meetings with underwriters
— full reviews of programme
— pressure on insurers in premium negotiations
— alternative quotations sought
— foreign

Intermediary attitudes
— who is responsible for the account? (status)
— meetings with senior executives

Insurer service
— loss statistics and in what form?
— claims handling and settlements
— administrative work direct with operating units (relationships)
— loss control surveys and advice (relationship with operators)
— any problems in service
— history of connection with insurer
— foreign

Insurer attitudes
— equitability of premiums
— posture adopted in premium negotiations
— understanding of activities and risks

Any areas of particular difficulty in buying insurance cover or adequate cover?

Extent of self-insurance
— domestic
— foreign
— structure and mechanisms including treatment or profit centres

History of self-insurance development

Analyses made and criteria adopted in deciding whether or not to self-insurance and the extent of self-insurance

System for recording self-insured losses
Premium payment system
— invoices
— operators pay to whom?
— premium allocation systems
— any multi-annual payments of individual premiums?

Recording system
- premiums
- insured claims
- deductibles
- recoveries
- fully self-insured losses including those fully within deductibles
- analyses undertaken

Incident reporting system (follow through from operators to insurer)
- insured losses
- uninsured losses
- possible future liability incidents
- extent and method of investigation
- claim forms used

Checks on outstanding insured claims
- how often?
- by whom?

Checks on insurers' reserves for o/s claims
- by whom?

Renewal system
- how issued?
- review by units or intermediaries and extent
- how thorough?
- how long before renewal date?

Systems and methods for monitoring activities and changes
- buildings and extensions
- vehicles and hirings
- machinery
- projects
- employees (bonding)
- new subsidiaries
- new processes or materials
- legal agreements
- money risk limits
- sprinkler turn-off
- any manual or other forms of instruction or operators

What internal circulars etc . . . do units receive on a formalised basis?

To what extent are field trips and visits made?
 — on demand from operators
 — at will by unit

Integration of units with planning and decision making
 — extent formalised

Any particular problems in keeping abreast of activities?
Method of property valuation
 — date of last base
 — valuation
 — indices used
 —- inflationary allowance

When were third party indemnities last reviewed/changed?
 — public
 — products
 — motor

How often are procedures reviewed?
 — extent of review

What reports and summaries are made upwards?
 — to whom?
 — content
 — how often?
 — copies if available

Any insurances handled for staff?
 — volume
 — system
 — schemes
 — directors and executives

Any insurances for outsiders?
 — volume and nature
 — how obtained and history
 — schemes
 — system
 — staff involved/cost/profit
 — loss control advice given
 — is there scope for increasing volume?
 — which insurers predominate?
 — professional negligence risk/insurance

Review filing system

Review daily input of paper and time involvement relative to importance

Changes made over recent years in units, systems, etc.

Ideas, grumbles, rejected plans etc. . . . .

Discuss insurance and self insurance in detail

— views on self-insurance
— ability to assume risk (annual)
— ability to assume risk (one loss)
— financial restraints
    (debenture trust deeds (full insurance clause etc?)
    (insurers as major stockholders or lenders
— non-financial restraints
— any factors peculiar to the organisation
    (e.g. public undertakings)

Checklist 2—Site Tour

LAYOUT BRIEFING (mark on plan)

Broad description of layout and processes
— basements
— feeder mains and sub-stations with areas served—
— protection
  ring mains
— standby power sources
— boilers (what used for?, fuels)
— tankage (contents, type)
— water (source, treatment plants)
— gas (lines, type, plant, storage)
— oil (storage)
— hazardous materials
— delivery points and vehicle routings
— storage locations for stocks
— raw materials
— finished goods
— flammables
— toxics
— gas cylinders
— spares stores
— workshops
— vehicle garages
— vehicle parks (accumulation risk)
— effluent treatment
— computers and terminals
— major control locations
— plants
— outflow
— solvent recovery
— laboratories
— ventilation plant
— PABX and telephone equipment
— fire mains and pumphouses, hydrants
— sprinklers etc. installations
— access and exits

Fire Areas

Injury Areas

Neighbours

Flood

Key areas and revenue dependencies

Key breakdown/damage items and what would be disastrous

External:
 Construction and Foundations
 Neighbouring hazards
 Fire Brigade Access—roads, obstructions
 General appearance—Housekeeping
 Fencing
 Hydrant Points
 FLT Operating Areas

Internal:
 Process 'eggs in one basket'
 Internal Construction/Separation
 Hazardous Materials
 Lighting
 Noise
 Vibration
 Dust
 Fumes
 Cleanliness
 Housekeeping
 Fire Points
 Safety Gear
 Notices
 Alarms
 Exits and Routes and to Where?
 Obstruction of Exits
 Obstruction of Emergency Equipment
 Manning
  — sex
  — age
  — nationality
 Work
  — content
  — sitting or standing
  — pace
  — dress and hazards

— guards and avoidance
Check a guard
Check a hose reel
Check extinguisher inspection labels
Fire separation

Checklist 3—Administrative

A major risk in the Financial and Administrative area is records loss

What is the extent of protection?
- accounts receivable
- unrecorded accounts receivable data
- wages records
- service and pension records
- EDP records and checks on their protection (bureau)
- any other key records?

Is there a high cash risk?
- transit
- transit security
- payroll make-up on site
- make up security
- pay-out procedure
- other cash handling
- cash security
- overnight risks
- distortions

What would be consequences of payroll loss
- if lost in transit?
- if lost after make-up?

Any history of fidelity loss?
- losses
- references
- those before engagement
- internal audit system

Is stock control a problem?
- attractiveness
- shortages

Are the office and its secrets considered as secure as necessary?

Taxation position
- legislation

- premium
- losses
- funds
- loss prevention

Ability to adjust cash-flow

Product Revenue and Gross Profits

- interest
- external
- overseas subsidiaries
- direct export
- location/area revenues and gross profits

Administrative structure (internal)

- units and locations
- personnel (with key names)
- functions
- reporting points (with names)
- relationships between the units
- foreign situation
- committees
  in a structure includes any subsidiaries for each:—
  date of establishment, where registered?, ownership,
  capital, profit and profit components and distribution
  and exact reasons for subsidiary.

Key personnel experience

- career histories
- any qualifications?
- any role or job descriptions?
- broad duties

Philosophy

- is there a financing policy/philosophy?
- written (copy)
- adopted by Board or financial executive
- date last revised
- how often reviewed?

Checklist 4—Transport and FLT Operation

What is make-up of fleet?
— on site
— off site
— any purpose built?
— self or contractor-operated?
— future charges

Nature of its work

Organisational structure
— management
— locations of depots and workshops
— in depots

Consider threats to the operation:
— accumulation risks
    fire, flood, aircraft, malicious persons
    number & type of vehicles
    effects of loss
    replacement time (new and secondhand)
    alleviating possibilities
— loss of any purpose built vehicles
    types, effects of loss
    replacement time (new and secondhand)
    alleviating possibilities
— contractor going out of business
    effects of loss, replacement time,
    alleviating possibilities
— accident risk — what is experience?
    damage costs
      collisions
      fires
      thefts
      in-depot damage
      damage by shunters etc.,
    loss of use costs
    accident rates and trends

— legal sanctions (e.g. Transport Act 1968 in U.K.)
  contractor operation possible?
  cost
  how many licensing authorities?
  proportions of each

Vehicle maintenance practices
— programmed or breakdown
— in-house or external
— checks on external work
— daily checks by drivers
  chits
  logged under driver heads
— tyre inspection and maintenance
— notices received under legislation
— records kept on vehicle maintenance
  effect of loss
  protection
— auditing maintenance
— mechanic shortages/turnover

Is there uniformity in vehicle maintenance and other aspects
of the fleet's operation, such as procedures on driver recruitment, training, accident prevention, etc., re laid down codes

Characteristics of driver force and job
— general experience of driver force
  difficulty in finding good material
  recruit — raw or experienced
  turnover
  age levels
— scope of drivers' job
  hours worked and overtime
  operating environment, extent of night work
— method of payment
  bonuses paid as earned or retained
— use of casuals
  ages, sources, seasonal
— industrial relations
  union difficulties
  action history
— references
  telephone, numbers checked, always done?
  letter, standard, copy, always done?

— medical checks
— photographs of driver
— identity cards
— explanation of safe driving, requirements & penalties
— probationary period
— variations for casual drivers

Extent of training in the fleet
— supervisors
    how?
    safety element
    what?
    follow up and refreshers
    programmed & logged
— drivers
    induction
    nature and content (safe driving/accident conduct)
    link with accident analysis
    how often?
    programmed and logged?
    any corrective training and retest procedure?
    what about casuals?
— management courses

Discuss driver supervision
— management/driver meetings
    how often?
    content
    safety included?
    accident performance
        (how often)
— any other communication of accident performance?
— transport newsheets etc.
— rules re carriage of passengers, giving lifts, stopping
    when hailed, leaving vehicles unattended, use of
    refreshment points, use of protected parks, im-
    mobilisation of vehicles, seal checks.
    action on breach?

What is driver recruitment procedure
— standard procedure
— who interviews?
— licence checks
    taking with convictions?

— use of application form
  who completes?
  copy
— driver test
  conducted by whom?
  use of check sheet
  road and yard?
— licence checks
  how often?
  holidays?
— who keeps licence?
— transport inspectors
— safety committees, awards, bonuses, etc.
— accident procedures
  who completes form?
  is it done with supervisor?
  any follow up interview? (with whom?)
  copy of claim form
  scene of accident aids in vehicles?
  where does claim form go?
— is there driver accident monitoring?
  system, disciplinary procedure
  drivers ever dismissed?

Any other statistical examination of accident performance
— unit accident performance monitoring
  system i.e. from depot or workshop returns or
  from central receiver of reports
  scope of statistics (copy)
  who examines and how often?
  action
  pressure exerted from top down on safety of
    operations?
— any target fixing?
— accident characteristic analyses
  system adopted (where done)
  utilisation
  any concrete results?
  if no analysis, probe experience knowledge

Vehicle features
— construction
  fibreglass?
  wooden bump boards?

— livery
— suitability for conditions/work
— cab design
— couplings
— lighting
— mirrors
— kerbing
— emergency equipment
— consultation with drivers on new vehicle designs
— washing routines

Insurance/vehicle repair practices
— when are assessors brought in?
— garages selected freely by selves?
— delays in getting repairs started?
— recovery of uninsured losses
— scope for self-insurance

Security aspects
— value and attractiveness of loads
— security devices on vehicles
— numbers removed from ignition switches?
— locks on delivery box vehicles
— methods of container sealing
        seal checks?
        tagging?
— marking on top of vehicles?
— radios
— how are open loads secured?
        nylon or traditional?
— trailer security devices re detachment

Other aspects
— route controls
        fixed?
        varied fixed?
        optional?
— any issue of written material to drivers?
— use of "please assist" cards to avoid drivers leaving
    breakdowns

Special safety programmes on FLT operations

Views on accident prevention
        cost aspects
        insurance aspects

F.L.T's.

F.L.T's. used
- — number
- — type
- — how propelled?
- — capacity
- — age
- — right for job?

Work of the F.L.T's.

Characteristics of driver force
- — general experience
   - difficulties in finding good material
   - recruit from raw or experienced
   - turnover
   - age levels
- — scope of drivers' job
   - hours worked and overtime
   - operating environment
   - extent of night work
- — method of payment
   - bonuses
   - piecework
- — use of casuals
   - ages
   - sources
   - seasonal
- — industrial relations
   - union difficulties
   - action history

Prevention of unauthorised use
- — licensing scheme?
- — key controls
   - lunchtime, overnight, drivers going to toilet
   - tea breaks etc . . . .

What happens when driver goes on holiday or sick?

- — spare drivers?
- — how often do they drive?

Maintenance of F.L.T.'s.
- — programmed or breakdown?

— in-house or external?
— checks on external work?
— driver checks
    chits?
    logged under driver heads?
— how long before faults dealt with?
— what happens when a truck is taken out of service?
    spares available?

Site Tour

General

    congestion
    tidiness
    route markings
    blind corners — what do drivers do?
    overhead hazards
    doors
    stacking
    pallet condition
    floor conditions — oil — slopes — things
    battery charging — impact — fire
    housekeeping controls
    sprinkler impairments

Pedestrians

    where do trucks operate intermixed with pedestrians
        (warehousemen — factory workers)?
    can it be avoided?
    turnover of new staff in these areas
    situations where a good establishment could be
        undone
    briefings to new and casual employees on FLT
        hazards
    how often to employees generally?

Trucks

    condition of tyres
    length of forks—pallets
    overhead protection and mesh
    hard hats?
    governors?
    hand trucks?
    gas — where are cylinders charged? — stored?

Driving

> high carrying
> horn use
> speed
> blind travelling
> loads right back?
> looking behind
> parked with forks lowered
> using reverse as a clutch?
> pedestrians
> smoking whilst operating
> sudden braking
> how close following?

Checklist 5—Marketing

Who are the customers?

Extent of demand
- — competition
- — revenue
- — gross profit

Any internal sales?
- — home
- — foreign (where?)
- — revenue

Any direct export sales
- — where?
- — revenue

Any seasonal features in production/or sales?

Any key customers?
- — exposures
- — effect of loss
- — % of revenue

Any major regional sales dependencies?

Other income
- — royalties
- — service

Effect of stoppage
- — on markets
- — lead time available
    finished goods stockpiles
    distributor stockpiles
    customer stockpiles
    aid from elsewhere in Group
    (capacities checked)

Rebuilding time in comparison

Additional aid possibilities
— aid from competitors
— foreign producers

Could risk be reduced through contingency planning?

Any interdependency exposures?
Selling activities
— salesmen
— advice and problem solving
— advertising
— importance of literature and aids
— exhibitions
— tests on third party property

Discuss HASAWA re products for use at work
— hazardous machinery etc.
— hazardous substances

Are standard sales conditions used?
— buyer
— copy

Discuss safeguarding product availability
— awareness of protecting raw materials and other
  supplies
— loss prevention on site
— product safety in development and production
— risk reviews in planning
— checks on suppliers, distribution, licences etc.

Any records which if lost would create difficulties?
— market statistics
— customer records
— special price records
— tender records
— protection (planned)

Marine exports CIF or other?
— write own certificates?

Marine damage costs
— analysis made?

Checklist 6—Personnel

What is personnel organisation?
— corporate
— operations

What are the characteristics of labour force?
— range of work
— hours and how paid? (bonus, piecework, etc. . . .)
— unions involved
  main craft unions
  main general unions
— is wage negotiation on national basis?
— are supervisors union members?
— supply of labour
  shortages
  bussing
  trends in skilled labour availability
— foreign workers (language problems)
— extent of overtime working

Consider major threats to the labour resource
— industrial action
  principal unions (if any)
— history of prevailing situation
  locations where likely to be most damaging
  machinery for early warning to trouble
  future factors
— riot
  history
  living conditions
  wage levels
  treatment
  improvements
  preparedness
  training for mangement in handling riot
  riot-prone situations
  checks for drunkenness
— epidemics
  possible epidemics
  likely effects

What about health risks?

— nature
    noise
    dust
    fumes
— monitoring situation
    hazardous materials problem
    writing to suppliers
    checking on new materials before commitment to
        buy/use
— briefing employees on hazards and protective gear
    supply and usage.

Are any medical examinations done on employees?

— at recruitment
    for whom
    how often? (programmed)
    scope
— scope of in-house medical/hygiene facilities
    extent of treatment given
    investigation of possible industrial illness
    cases

Discuss employee accident, prevention practices (refer 'Employee Safety')

What about training?

How are employees trained? — is there a formalised approach?

— general employees
    induction (safety — what?)
    job training (how?)
    safety content of job training (are there working
        procedures for each job)
    link with accident analysis
    logging
— supervisors
    what?
    how?
    safety element (positive or negative)
    follow up and refreshers
    logging
— general safety training
    management

      supervisors
      operatives
      content
      how often?
      programmed?
— any special programmes?
      vehicles
      F.L.T's.
      crane drivers
      electrical

Do employees work abroad?
— temporarily
      nature of work
      periods
      any to North America?
— secondments to foreign interests
      does subsidiary employ and pay wages?
      periods involved
      nature of work

Any secondments into this country?
      who pays employee?
      periods involved
      nature of work

Any use of direct labour?

Any records which if lost would create difficulty?
— nature
— protection

Key personnel and travel safeguards

Kidnap exposure and precautions

Checklist 7—Computer

What is computer used for?
— own, leased or bureau?
— location
— type of machine
— working hours
— batch or real time?

Effect of machine loss on operations
— stoppage, inconvenience, increased cost, etc . . . . .
    (postponability)
— back-up plan
— test runs (last)
— compatibility problems
— if no plan, how common are similar machines in
    area? Capacity
— if plan, is there also planning for getting it into
    motion? (e.g. Saturday night fire)

What about records protection?
— data
— programmes (object and source files)
— systems manuals
— documentation
    how strict is documentation
    work in progress documentation
— unprocessed batches
— spot checks on records protection

Is there a formalised security plan for the computer facility?
— access to computer area
— access to computer room
— references on employment
— action on dismissals
— access to computer data on-line
— stationery access

Do third parties ever operate the computer?
— from where?
— purpose

— how often?

Is there protection against loss of air conditioning or power?
- separate air conditioning unit and standby
- standby power
- fixed fire protection
- maintenance

Is there any emergency training for employees?
- fire extinguisher training
- how often?
- new employees

Is bureau work done for third parties?
- nature (any systems analysis, programme design etc.)
- batch or real time?
- protection of data (incl. unprocessed batches)
- copy of conditions

Copies of contracts with outside bureau

Computer area inspection
- what around, above and below?
- contruction materials
- firewalls surround from real floor to real floor above.
- separate processors in separate rooms
- minimum outside glass
- non-combustible furniture and fixtures
- no unnecessary water or steam pipes (including in area above)
- is floor above watertight?
- real floor positive drainage
- airtight glazing
- protected and screened cable openings
- floor panels accessible and marked
- cleanliness in under floor areas
- separate storage rooms for paper stock
- no electrical transformers in computer room
- no air ducts passing through
- coolant systems alarmed

Any entry to third party computer facilities?
- operation of machines
- controls

Checklist 8—Employee Safety

What is the injury experience?
— main types
— trends
— particular problem areas

How are accidents reported and investigated?
— who investigates?
— first aid incidents
— near-miss incidents
— how recorded and analysed?
— link with training
— copies of forms and statistics

U.K.

How are the requirements of Health and Safety At Work Act being met or were they already met? — is there a Statement of Policy?
— copy of policy
— is responsibility formally allocated other than on policy?
— safety representatives
   who?
   training
— safety committees
   who?
   how often?
   what do they (it) do?
   injury only or all classes of loss?
   any instructions given?
   minuted?
— any other consultations, for example, on new plant materials or processes?
— informing employees on new hazards

Foreign

Any formal definition of attitudes to safety and responsibility for safety?
— how (policy or otherwise)?

— injury or all classes of loss?
— if policy, a copy

Any safety committees, representatives or similar units concerned with safety?
— who?
— what are duties (defined)?
— injury or all classes of loss?

Laws affecting safety

Any safety inspection systems or procedures?
— supervisor inspections
  planned
  check lists
  extent
  monitoring
— insurers/brokers
— government inspectors
— fire and emergency gear

Risk reviews in planning and change
Discuss job training

— general employees
  induction (safety — what?)
  job training (how?)
  safety content of job training (are there working
    procedures for each job?)
  link with accident analysis
  logging
— supervisors
  what?
  how?
  safety element (positive or negative)
  follow up and refreshers
  logging

General safety training
— management
— supervisors
— operatives
— content
— how often?
— programmed?

Special programmes
 — vehicles
 — F.L.T's.
 — crane drivers
 — electrical maintenance personnel

Any first aid training
 — number qualified

Is personal protective gear important?
 — what?
 — supply
 — response

Any particular health hazards?
 — sources and identification
 — environmental monitoring

What medical facilities on hand?
 — extent
 — response to emergency
 — getting people out of difficult situations
 — medical checks on employees
 — medical job specifications

Any use of toxic materials?
 — nature and identification
 — controls
      delivery
      storage
 — safety showers etc.

Briefing to employees on health hazards and toxic materials

What is the reaction to accidents of safety performance?
 — is there accountability in this area?
 — does management see accident figures?
      how often?
      in what form?
      reaction
 — is there any direction or pressure from above?
 — any injury figures monitored?
      by whom?

What is the view on Health and Safety At Work Act?

What is the view on cost of accidents?
— could accidents be considered as a major cost item?

Any system of safety rules, competitions, targets etc.?

If safety officer also discuss
— width of role.
  If all losses, cover records protection, contingency
  planning, handling of complaints, monitoring product
  safety, contract controls, pollution, overall reviews,
  and management education.
— whom he reports to
— particular problems
  (staffing etc).

Checklist 9—Legal

Any particular features of the law adding to or subtracting from liability risk?
— absence of common law
— contracting out of liability—enforceable?
— impositions of absolute liability and 'no fault'
— safety legislation (fire injury, pollution, products, machinery inspection)
— directors' and officers'
— workmen's compensation

*To what extent is liability law known and used?
— propensity and ability of individuals to sue (legal aid)
— propensity of corporations to sue
— damages levels for individuals and corporations
— trends in climate
— influence of unions
— professional negligence

Any particular activities adding to liability?

How are public complaints and claims handled?

— acknowledgements
— procedure
— briefing to employees and management on how to deal with complaints and claims

To what extent are standard conditions used?
— use controls
— variance controls (salesmen)
— acceptance of supply conditions
— acceptance of others conditions
— checking new standard conditions
— signing of indemnities by employees

Any special statutes affecting operations?

Any involvement in new product development?

*foreign investigations only

Any legal staff in field?

*What is developing in the law?
- — pollution
- — damages
- — professional negligence
- — product law
- — no fault
- — workmen's compensation

Is there system for communicating new legislative developments to field?

Is there a protection system on important legal documents and records?
- — titles and deeds
- — case data

*foreign investigations only

Checklist 10—Property

Range of properties
— owned properties
public buildings or similar high-rise properties
unusual properties
— leased properties
range
public buildings or similar
high-rise properties
unusual properties
controls
extent of insurance checks where insured by lessor.

Any leasing-out?
— types of property (including sub-lets on leased
properties)
— controls
can anyone lease out or grant a tenancy?
standard lease or tenancy agreement (copies)
variance controls
sub-letting controls re occupancy risks
risk and insurance position
— checks on insurance if/when left to others
— rental income
any properties producing high proportion of income?

Extent of hazard analysis on new properties
— own properties
design and pre-occupation
extent
by whom?
any architectural codes
— pre-leasing or agreeing a tenancy
(by whom?)

Discuss day to day management and supervision of properties and particularly safety and security practices
— location of responsibility
— organisation:

fire alarm checks
fire exit checks
evacuation drills
bomb scares
hazardous defects reported or found
cupboards and basements
checks on tenancies
checks on contractors
by whom?
laid down and on a programmed basis?
logged?
— night and week-end security
(contractors or own employees?)
— what about leased-out buildings, where managed?
— any fire prevention requirements in leasing out or
tenancy agreements?
notifying proposed changes
action taken re hazard checks

Any hazard checks on proposed changes by selves?
— by whom?
— contractor checks

Other risks associated with properties

Any concession rentals?
nature
special arrangements re safety of people on public
property
— shared occupancies with others—t.p. risk
nature of work done
nature of other occupancies

Discuss property valuations
— base used—how developed?
— indices used for up-dating
— inflationary allowance

Discuss scope for selective basis of insured values
— computerised asset register
— singling out non-replacement properties

Discuss future developments in property

Any records which if lost would cause any difficulty?
— nature
— protection

Checklist 11—Product Development and Quality Control

DEVELOPMENT

Extent of product development

Extent to which product safety is considered in the development process.
- — checks on legal standards
- — review of claims and complaints on similar products (including literature searches)
- — prototypes and labelling attention
- — Instructions and labelling attention (including legal check)
- — packaging included?
- — action since HASAWA

Are manufacturing and transit hazards considered too?

Is there monitoring of claims and complaints on products already in market for future implications?
- — action
- — reference during design

Is there involvement in the selection of suppliers for new products?
- — checks on premises

Is there liaison with quality control?

What records are important to product development?
- — documentation of tests (how long?)
- — vital research data
- — final formula or specifications
- — protection

Effect of loss of research facility
- — recovery and alleviating possibilities

Any vital laboratory equipment?
— replacement problems

Any health hazards to development personnel?
— medical surveillance

Are products for export made to same standard?
— instructions and labelling translations
— what is left to foreign units?
New products notified to insurance organisation

QUALITY CONTROL

Range of Existing Products

Liability Potential

Extent of quality/safety checks in manufacturing process (all or sample basis?)
— raw materials checks
— consumables checks
— packaging checks
— finished product checks
— factory checks
— literature monitoring

Is there a laboratory clearance requirement before materials drawn from stocks?

Is the legal situation monitored, e.g., HASAWA and checks on existing products?

Is there a check on other peoples goods for re-sale?
How are complaints and claims handled?

What is the procedure?
— acknowledgement
— who is notified?
— investigation
— consideration of implications for product recall and instructions
— briefing to employees on handling claims and complaints
— can a product be checked back to batch?
— can the checks on the batch or product be traced?
— how long are check records kept?

— volume of complaints and injuries
— any serious?
— potential

Is QC involved in the selection of suppliers?
— checks on suppliers premises before selection
— action

Are there any particular hazards to QC staff?
— injury
— health
— medical monitoring

Effect of loss of QC facility
— recovery and alleviating possibilities

Any vital laboratory equipment?

What records are important to the QC function?
— test records
— complaints and investigations records
— how long kept?
— protection

Are there any licensee manufacturers?
— do they do anything to products?
— inspections, scope and action
— instruction on claims and complaints
— is there feed-back on these?
— same standards as products made here?

Review of QC system and practices

Checklist 12—Fire and Security

What has been the experience?
- — where?
- — causes

Any particular hazards?

Range of extinguishing equipment
- — hand extinguishers and hose reels
- — sprinklers
- — other systems
- — site fire brigade (strength and duties)
- — explosion alleviation

How is alarm raised and carried through?
- — alarm points
- — phones (check night situation)
- — radios
- — smoke and other detection systems

How far is public fire brigade? (time)
- — traffic congestion
- — strength and equipment
- — liaison
- — visits to site
- — have plan of relevant items?
- — involvement in new plans?

Any (what is) planned approach to dealing with outbreaks?
Is there an evacuation procedure?
- — drills (last), notices, disabled persons
- — employee training in reaction to fires and use of equipment (whom? when? and refreshers)
- — alarm procedures checks
- — major emergency plan (scope, drill, review)

What checks on emergency equipment?
- — extinguishers and hose reels
- — hydrants
- — alarms and alarm systems

- sprinklers (obstruction, dust on heads etc.)
- sprinkler valves
- explosion alleviation
- how often?
- by whom?
- check list of items and locations
- programmed check on contracted inspections?

What water supplies are available?
- nature
- mains diameter
- pressure
- pressure tests (how often?)

MOVING ON TO PREVENTION RATHER THAN CURE

What general fire prevention inspections are made?
- brokers and insurers (how often?)
- supervisors (how often?) (check lists?)
- fire officer, committees etc.
- external areas and roadways

Any procedures for checking fire exits and routes?

Is there a 'close-down' procedure?

How is rubbish and waste dealt with? (housekeeping)

Are there fire protection reviews on new building plans?
- by whom?
- before commitment

What about new plant, processes and materials?

Any large use of flammable liquids on site?
- what? (nature)
- delivery
- storage
- handling
- identification

Is there a permit system on fire prone work such as welding?
- procedure
- supervision and fire readiness

What about the recording and analysis of fires?
- copies

— recording costs (management knowledge)

Is there any management education on fire and fire prevention?
(If a fire officer, to whom does he report?)

Security manning on site
— numbers
— main concerns and duties

Access and exit controls
— visitors
— employees
— vehicles
— administrative offices
— laboratories

Site non/low working times and patrol routines
Experience of theft (anything attractive?)
— stock
— equipment
— transit
— costs (management knowledge)

Any items on site which, if stolen, could disrupt operations?
— what? (electrodes, key moulds etc . . .)
— protection

Any experience of arson and sabotage?

Any experience of riot or near-riots?
— preparedness
— training for management in handling riot prone situations
— propensity to riot (labour conditions etc.)
— checks for drunkenness (foreign)

Is there a security officer?
— cash in transit
— payroll make-up security
— office security
— computer security
— valve security
— key equipment security
— particular problems and any difficulties in getting security attention from management?
— to whom does he report?

Checklist 13—Purchasing

Raw Materials

Consumables

Is a standard purchasing order used? (copy)
— supplier conditions risks, including delivery notes

Look at some supplier conditions

Any purchasing outside purchasing function?

Any records which if lost would create difficulty?
— stock records
— source records
— any other key records
— protection

Insurance on marine consignments (CIF or C & F)

Damage to consignments
    cost
    analysis
    scope for t.l.o.

Checklist 14—Engineering

Check site layout (plan)

Broad explanation of the process
— origins, age, uniqueness of plant
— if self-made, ability to replace in event of major loss
— also if self-made or designed, the protection of specifications
— rebuilding time and distortions which could arise

Key breakdown/damage items (what would be disastrous?)
— key spares held
— monitored lead times on high turnover items
— location
— single building or split?
— if split, is this by type?
— effect of spares holding loss
   help from elsewhere in Group
help from rest of industry
foreign suppliers

What energy and other consumables is site dependent on?
— power (sources, feeders, importance and protection aspects, any joint points on public and standby?)
— fuel (nature, sources, multiple sourcing, transport, stocks in time, importance and effect of stock loss)
— water (sources, transport, treatment, importance, protection aspects and stocks, effect of impaired water and monitoring for this)
— gas (nature, sources, transport, importance, protection aspects and stocks)
— steam (importance and protection aspects)
— other (packaging, catalysts, electrodes, solvents, etc.)
— any from inside Group?

Are vehicles and mobile plant important?
— on-site (effect of loss and replacement aspects)
— off-site (effect of loss and replacement aspects)
— accumulation risks

231

How important is day to day maintenance?
— organisation
— preventive—hazardous items too or just critical ones?
— time lag—pressure on resources
— getting money
— earth testing
— plant and vehicle inspections
— lifting gear inspection (including chains and slings)

To what extent do supervisors and employees report hazardous defects as opposed to things which affect working?
— chit system
— labelling system
— priority system on hazardous defects
— encouragement in training or otherwise to report defects

Does new equipment receive a safety check before coming into use?
— by whom?
— is there a formal procedure?
— 'no-use' label
— clearance chit to supervisor
— before purchase

What about new buildings, processes and materials?
Is a standard purchasing order used on new equipment? (copy)
— supplier conditions risks, including delivery notes

Is all equipment ordering through the engineering function?
— violations of safety check procedure

What about contract engagements—are these all through engineering?
— what contract conditions are used?
— top limits
— contract signed before start of work?
— insurances checked before start of work?
— safety briefing and rules

Is there a similar situation with small/casual contractors?

What sort of supervision on contractors during work?

Any weekend or out of shift contractor or engineering work?

Any 'permit system' on fire prone work such as welding?
— procedure
— supervision and fire readiness

Any plant hiring — in or out?
— conditions applied

Any records which if lost would create difficulty?
— site drawings
— machine specifications
— spares index/stock lists/suppliers
— maintenance programme data
— protection

Any use of computers?

Valve and key equipment security

Is there any dependency on moulds or patterns?
— importance and effect of loss
— protection

Any future changes on site?
— layout
— plant
— technology

Checklist 15—Emergency Planning

General

Extent of formal plans for dealing with incidents (obtain copies)

How were they drawn up?
— checked with all key persons
— checked with relevant public authorities
— checked with sources of help

Is everyone involved given briefing on plants and pocket copies of their own duties?

Are new employees (including those transferred from other parts of company) issued with copies of fire instructions on arrival?

Are contractors, cleaning staff, etc?

Training in special emergency duties e.g. searching for bombs

Posting of fire instructions and other procedures

Language of these and other signs relative to languages of work force

Are test exercises conducted and how often?

How long to evacuate?

Is there programmed review of the plans and by whom?

Do fire brigade have a plan of plant showing location of fire fighting and emergency equipment, hazards, materials, etc., and details of manning?

Is the copy kept in gatehouses and by key personnel?

Are evacuation wardens or similar provided with identifying markers?

Are incident controllers and do they have special communications facilities?

Are evacuation check points provided with stands and prominently signed?

If there is a gas leak risk have alternative check points been earmarked and procedures established for suitable direction of employees to correct one in circumstances prevailing?

Extent of any business interruption planning
— copies
— how drawn up?
— review

Telephonists' training and instructions:
— on receiving emergency calls

Written plans check
Fire instructions to employees
— finding a fire
— nature of alarm and action required
— names of wardens
— loss reduction

Extent to which plans cover different types of incident
— bomb scares, major strikes and commotions, pollution and product leakage

How is 'emergency' declared? (n.b. different types requiring different procedures)

Duties of individuals stated including special duties
Provision for 'at scene' controller and 'general' controller and listing of several alternatives
— prompt sheets

Provision for verifying states of plant manning when incident occurs

Telephonists' instructions on dealing with 'bomb scare' calls
— have they written copies of these instructions?

Necessary contacts in company or elsewhere listed with day and night telephone numbers

Sources of possible outside help listed with day and night telephone numbers

Is emergency equipment and its whereabouts logged?

Is there provision for incidents at or involving ancillary distant property connected with plant such as pipeline leaks, vehicle accidents, rail tank cars, etc.?

Provision for
— shepherding and checking out employees
— evacuating disabled staff
— evacuating and checking out visitors and other non-employees
— closing fire doors
— vehicles and transport generally
— meeting and directing brigade
— providing brigade with important information
— dealing with press
— canteen facilities
— movement of emergency equipment to incident site
— dealing with calls to plant including customers
— salvage work
— first aid and medical staff
— security during incident
— warnings to neighbouring plants if necessary
— informing key personnel elsewhere in company
— public safety and sightseers
— notifying 'head office'

INDEX

237